T0386303

THE CAPPELLINI METHOD.
A PERFORMING DREAM

FRANCESCA SERRAZANETTI

Electa

I wish to dedicate this book to all those who
supported me in the moments of great victories
and in the times of great defeats. And I also wish
to dedicate it to all those unsavory characters
who say that design is not getting us anywhere.
A big Bronx cheer to these people and a big
"bravo" instead to all the men and women
who taught and assisted me, ensuring I grew
in the world of design, and above all those
who helped me realize that the key point
is to try and make people smile and dream.

Giulio Cappellini

To Silvia, Costanza, Giovanni and Margherita
Pilar, who support me and bear with me
day by day: thank you so much.

Desidero dedicare questo libro a tutti coloro
che mi hanno sostenuto nei momenti di grandi
vittorie e nei momenti di grandi sconfitte.
E desidero anche dedicarlo a tutti quei personaggi
"poco raccomandabili" che dicono che tanto con il
design non si va da nessuna parte.
Una grande pernacchia a queste persone ed un
grande "Bravo" invece a tutti gli uomini e le
donne che mi hanno risegnito, aiutato e fatto
crescere nel mondo del design e, soprattutto, che
mi hanno fatto capire che la cosa fondamentale
è cercar di far sorridere e sognare le persone.

KEY

IDENTITY

ENCOUNTERS

EXHIBITING DESIGN

PROCESSES

CONTENTS

A PERFORMING DREAM

G iulio Cappellini's is a life
of encounters, objects and great
dreams to be fulfilled. The same
goes for his company, its identity
shaped by a strong sense
of innovation that combines
creativity, internationalization, avant-garde
ideas and crafts skills. Cappellini's journey through
the design universe began in the late seventies:
a quest that took him to different continents
to discover whatever was going on around the world
and open up the borders of Italian production.
A journey undertaken with the curiosity and
tenacity of one who wanted to create the identity
of a project with experimentation in design
as its watchword. In this way a network of young
talents, internationally based and often unknown,
was created. The only skill necessary was to have
something to say to achieve the common goal.
Design has first of all to convey feelings and
enter people's homes.

Cappellini is not only a contemporary furniture
business: it is a workshop of ideas, an all-round
project that has succeeded in exploring and
mapping new cultural trends, discovering talents
like Jasper Morrison or the Bouroullec brothers,
creating objects with a strong and refined identity,
trying to respond to people's innermost desires
while being unfailingly innovative.

This story takes the form of a "scrapbook"
of personal memories, extraordinary encounters,
projects and ideas, a mix of fantasy and reality.
There is no need to follow a conventional
narrative, and with the freedom to explore
what lies behind this important piece
of design history, readers can seek their own
key to the secrets of the Cappellini method.
A method that has been built out of rigor and
at the same time freedom, coherence of ideas and
the contradictions of creativity. This is reflected
in the book's structure: a word list that combines
proper nouns and common nouns, arranged

in alphabetical order, a system that presents a strict sequence but is, at the same time, flexible in terms of meanings and the ways it can be read. As a deeply rich expression of a cultural value, the alphabetical entry thus becomes part of the most basic structure in the world, recalling the dictionary and the encyclopedia, as well as the simplicity of a child's spelling book.

From the entries there emerge some strong cross-cutting themes, which offer a new order of alternate reading to an alphabetical or temporal sequence. The *encounters* with the people who have shaped the history of Cappellini, including designers, and the cultural collaborations, those unfulfilled and those still in the bud. The *identity* of a company distinguished by the strength of a cultural project, which not only works on the product but also on the contents, with a sensibility that is open to different fields of knowledge and creativity, but art above all. The stress laid on the forms

and ways in which it chooses to *exhibit design* with installations that bring it closer to people and immerse visitors in the domestic dimension of a living environment, unexpected and welcoming. The *processes* that accompany the development of the products, with the emphasis on experimentation, R&D, multiculturalism and a product range whose specific features reflect the contrasts between craft and industry, the wisdom of "making" and advanced technology, manual skills and research.

The result that emerges is a "novel about things," which can be freely reassembled by the reader, one capable of recounting Giulio Cappellini's creative parabola by articulating stories, memories and visions. One every page of this book, entry after entry is woven out of principles of method, memories, passions, stories of objects, encounters and exhibitions that have marked and guided the creation of a major project: a dream that is here embodied in words and pictures.

ARCHITETTURA, L'INIZIO

ARCHITECTURE, BEGINNINGS

Michele De Lucchi, *Tavolo Tecnico* for Cappellini International (1987): a simple mechanism raises and lowers the top, which remains horizontal.

G iulio Cappellini always thought he would be an architect. As a child he played with Lego and Meccano. Growing up, he enrolled in the School of Architecture at the Milan Polytechnic, fascinated by the great architectural works of his legends as a student, like Mies van der Rohe and Gio Ponti.

He did his first work experience under Gio Ponti. "A year in his office," he now says, "did more for me than five years at university. This great eclectic, great artist, great architect and great designer, taught me that nothing can be left to chance and that each project has to be cherished from beginning to end, like a child."

One evening he told his parents he did no longer wanted to be an architect, but to take over a small company that had been founded by his father Enrico in 1946. A family business that for the past thirty years had been turning out furniture. Giulio wanted to convert it at once into a landmark for international design.

It was 1977 and alongside Cappellini was Rodolfo Dordoni, his companion at university. Together they began to create the first designs, like the *Colombia* containers or *Aliante* bookcases, and tried to give the business a new direction. They started by involving various Italian architects, such as Franco Raggi and Michele De Lucchi, who designed the first products in the catalogue, before the brand expanded internationally.

So the company was, in fact, refounded by Giulio Cappellini, in a small town close to Milan in the late seventies, when the city housed the offices of designers like Ettore Sottsass and Vico Magistretti and had one of the most important trade **fairs** as well as publishers and specialist journals. The Milan that was already becoming the city of industrial design, a nerve center and landmark for companies and designers around the world.

If you ask him about the relationship between architecture and design today, Cappellini answers: "Architects are not always good designers, designers are not always good architects. In some cases they are (think of Mies). In other cases the change of scale generates a lot of bad products. I think it's a question of sensibility. Design should not be seen as less important than architecture."

ARTE COME ISPIRAZIONE

ART AS INSPIRATION

A —

rt is perhaps Giulio Cappellini's greatest passion. It exerts a powerful influence over his approach to design. He views art, searches for it and explores it wherever he travels and at major **fairs** around the world, from Art Basel to Design Miami. He also looks for it in the smaller galleries of the various lesser towns he visits on his many travels, seeking new talents, initiating new partnerships, or simply satisfying his unfailing curiosity.

An art lover and collector of established artists and promising young unknowns, his artistic interests reveal a breadth of taste and that attraction of opposites typical of his choices in design. Just think of his two great passions, Jean-Michel Basquiat and Lucio Fontana: Basquiat's expressive and hypertrophic energy, richly detailed and ironical, inspired by children's drawings, in contrast with Fontana's minimalism, working by paring away everything superfluous to attain a synthesis and supreme rarefaction.

In Cappellini's world, the influences between art and design have been embodied in different forms over the years, transmitted by encounters and research projects. The projects are definitely not commercial, but they have had a significant impact on the company's growth in terms of image and a more international vision. This goes back to the "Cappellini Art" series launched in the late eighties with Romeo Gigli and Carla Sozzani, with exhibitions devoted to artists with widely different identities and from different backgrounds, such as Kim MacConnel, Aldo Mondino, Izhar Patkin or Kris Ruhs, who also produced a **limited edition** for Cappellini. Art became a part of the **exhibition** in the company's **showrooms** and spaces, and influenced many objects with its forms, textures, proportions and colors. If the Cappellini containers are inspired by Donald Judd's minimalist art, their fluo colors evoke light installations by Dan Flavin. Then the Cappellini catalogue contains some products reissued as actual tributes to artists, like the cabinets designed by Shiro **Kuramata** in 1975 and reissued in 2009 with a lacquer black vertical lines on white, red, yellow and blue grounds, homage to the most graphic works by the master of neoplastic art Piet Mondrian.

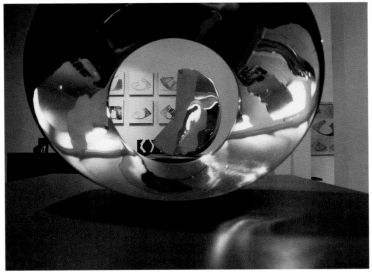

Angelo Mangiarotti, *The DNA
of sculpture*, Spazio Cappellini,
Milan, 1999.

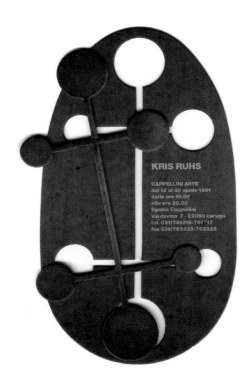

KRIS RUHS

CAPPELLINI ARTE
dal 12 al 20 aprile 1991
dalle ore 10.00
alle ore 22.00
Spazio Cappellini
via cavour 7 - 22060 carugo
tel. 031/761318-761717
fax 031/763333-763322

Kris Ruhs, "Cappellini Arte,"
Spazio Cappellini, Carugo,
1991. Invitation and photos
of the exhibit design.

Above: *Venetian Glass,
exhibition of vases and Murrine*,
"Cappellini Arte," Spazio
Cappellini, Carugo, 1991.

Opposite: *Kim MacConnel*,
"Cappellini Arte," Spazio
Romeo Gigli, Milan, 1989.

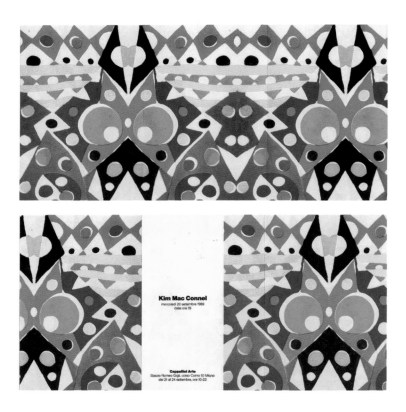

Kim MacConnel, "Cappellini
Arte", Spazio Romeo Gigli,
Milan, 1989.

AZAMBOURG

François Azambourg, *Mr. B* (2006).

"N ot a designer in the conventional sense of the term, but an inventor of materials and forms." So Giulio Cappellini describes François Azambourg, one of the leaders of the French movement of contemporary home design, whose name has been connected with the Italian company since 2005. An absolutely eclectic character, he not only designs objects but creates evocative forms by experimenting with unusual techniques, working on new technologies and finding uses for recycled materials.

The meeting between Cappellini and Azambourg took place in Paris in 2005 at an exhibition sponsored by VIA (Valorisation de l'Innovation dans l'Ameublement—a French association for fostering design), as part of Carte Blanche, where he had exhibited a chair in crumpled blue sheet metal (the blue of Bugatti cars). This prototype gave rise to the idea of creating a series of chairs, armchairs and stools named *Mr. B*.

The essential principle underlying the fabrication of this collection consists of injecting polyurethane foam into metal profiles, shaping and modifying the mold, so creating pieces on an industrial scale but which seem to be one-off products. The firm developed the technique through a long process of engineering, testing and verification, which led to a progressive refinement of the initial idea. The end result is a chair with an innovative tactile sensation, wedding lightness to the structural strength of steel.

The process of **production** of Bugatti chairs goes through several stages. The sheet metal is first laser-cut and then crumpled by being beaten by hand. The shapes are then bent, welded, sanded, polished, galvanized and painted. Then the inner core is injected with polyurethane. Its presence inside the metal shell eliminates the sounding-board effect of the hollow structure and also

prevents it from being deformed by the user's weight while remaining extraordinarily light (about 1.7 kg). The seat is then painted like a car, not only in the Bugatti blue of the first edition, but also variations in Ferrari red, Lamborghini yellow, Rolls-Royce black and Fiat gray.

The analysis of the production mode of this collection highlights the scope of the results achieved in terms of engineering from a single product, and is characteristic of the complexity of the firm's work. In static/structural terms, the difficulties associated with the stability of the chair have been solved by design choices that have made only very slight aesthetic/formal variations. The irregularity of the surface of the sheet metal constituted another level of difficulty, both for welding (since the exoskeleton has to be hermetically sealed around the injected polyurethane) and the painting. Both points were dealt with by a first phase of spot welding alternating with electric conduction, welding of internal and perimetric reinforcements, and with the inclusion of important phases of grinding, galvanizing and retouching of the welds. Electrolytic galvanizing baths identified all the micro-holes so they could be removed and the metal sheet was made resistant to atmospheric agents.

Mr. B is a family of objects that is a good example of Cappellini's concern with **post-industrial** production. They are manufactured industrially but with a technology that allows the product to be embellished by differentiating every single piece, with a final hand-crafted finish.

It may seem no more than a detail, but it is this factor that turns the simple metal chairs into extremely complex and interesting objects, an idea that stems from the use of products in everyday life. Sheet metal, subjected to daily use, soon gets marked and spoilt, so why not create a sheet metal object that is already crumpled? The defect becomes a peculiar characteristic and acquires a particularly decorative potential.

The *Mr. B* series in color variants Bugatti blue, Ferrari red, Rolls-Royce black and Lamborghini yellow.

BOUROULLEC

Ronan and Erwan Bouroullec,
Cloud bookcase (2004).

It all started in Paris in 1998 over a cigarette. At the Salon du Meuble, Giulio Cappellini eyed the first project by Ronan, the elder of the Bouroullec brothers, at that time not yet joined with his young brother Erwan in an artistic and business partnership. It was the *Cuisine désintégrée,* a prototype that featured a new model of fitted kitchen, which completely overturned the canons of the classic American kitchen. It suggested making a break with the idea of "made to measure" and conceiving the kitchen not as a room, but a simple structure, whose various pieces of equipment became a laboratory space. A piece of furniture based on the idea of flexibility, easily mounted and detached from the wall, such as a table that can be moved and which does not have to be left behind when the family moves house. "I asked the organizer to introduce me to this young designer," says Cappellini. "After I'd been waiting for a while he didn't turn up so I asked him what happened. They said he was nervous about meeting me and had gone out for a smoke. I replied there was no problem, I'm a smoker, so I joined him. We smoked together and got talking about things we could do together."

The luck (and merit) of catching Giulio Cappellini's eye marked a turning point in the Bouroullec brothers' career. Thanks to him their first projects to be produced industrially won them an international reputation. Cappellini tells how stimulating it is to do projects with them: "One has a more poetic soul, while the other is more closely engaged with production systems and technology. They work in a constructive partnership that fosters their contrasting personalities, but with a shared ideal of balance and refinement. They're among the most interesting designers on the market today, because their every project embodies little surprises both in the use of materials and formal expression. They offer an extremely light and evocative vision of design that enters **people**'s hearts, because they're neither rigid nor remote."

The *Lit Clos,* based on a similar principle to the kitchen, is a "micro-architecture" capable of performing various functions, characterizing and diversifying the spaces in which it is placed. It was one of the first projects by the Bouroullec brothers that Cappellini presented at the Milan furniture fair in 2000. Conceived on a scale halfway between a bed and a room, raised from the ground to evoke a tree house or Bruno Munari's *Abitacolo*, it presented a new way of secluding the sleeping area for

Cloud bookcase in a 2004
advertisement photo, showing
a composition of five modules.

a person who lives, works and often sleeps
in the same room. The same year the *Spring*
chair was also presented. This was a system
of elements in polyurethane foam padding
covered in leather or fabric (the shell
of the seat, footrest and headrest) which can
be combined to compose four different types
of seats. It was followed by the *Hole* chair
in aluminum, the console tables made of Corian®
with a mirror or planter and built-in tray,
the *Butterfly* containers, the *Basketball* sofa and
the **Progetto Oggetto** collection of objects,
such as a wooden fruit bowl, the "skeletons"
of acrylic lamps, and some vases. But there
were also other products not in the catalogue,
such as the *Samurai* chair or *Glide* sofa, which
again modulated the spaces of the home
by combining into a single object a series
of functions of the living room (shelves, sofa,
chaise longue). And again the *Brick* shelves,
a modular system built by simply sending out
a print file, which enables them to be laser cut.

The double-sided bookcase *Cloud* became
an icon of the Cappellini catalogue. It can be
interpreted as a natural evolution of the *Brick*
system. It is a "cloud" in white polyethylene
with see-through compartments. They are
produced as modular units that can be combined
endlessly using pressure clips. Produced

in 2004, it was the first large object the firm
made by rotational molding a plastic material.
This process manufactures hollow bodies
as single pieces without welding, turning
out elements devoid of internal tensions and
of uniform thickness. *Cloud* is further testimony
to Cappellini's capacity for technical innovation.
Starting with a very precise design, he created
the mold that would turn out the finished
piece with all the necessary features. The mold
is filled manually by pouring in the plastic
matter, in powder or liquid form. Once closed
it is rotated in a heated chamber, so that
the polymer melts and is deposited uniformly
on all the walls. Rotation continues during
cooling to keep the shape as the piece solidifies.
Finally, the piece is extracted. The special
feature of this technology lies in the fact that
the rotation takes place on a primary axis,
in a fixed direction, and with a secondary, variable
direction. The polymer is fused by heating
and the double movement ensures it coats all
the inner surfaces of the mold evenly. Hence
this technique does not exploit centrifugal force,
but fusion in contact with the walls.

Cloud is yet another demonstration that each
product has its own history, not only formal but
also productive, a mix of craftsmanship
and technology.

January 13, 1998: the first fax sent by Giulio Cappellini to Ronan Bouroullec after their meeting at the Salon du Meuble in Paris.

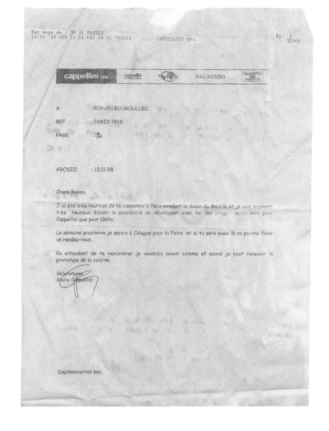

February 23, 1998, Paris-Milan: with a plane ticket sent him by Cappellini, Ronan Bouroullec travels to Milan for a meeting at the Carugo office.

Following pages: Ronan and Erwan Bouroullec, *Lit Clos* (2000) with *Hole* chairs (1999), *Brick* bookcase (2000) and *Zip Carpet* (2001).

CAFFÈ, 500, CHAMPAGNE

COFFEE, 500, CHAMPAGNE

B lack and no sugar. A good (and beautiful) cup of coffee is a must. To start the day right or enjoy a break, but also as part of a total, open-ended, free and eclectic design. One of the fundamental traits of Cappellini's character has always been eclecticism, in the belief that openness and versatility are essential to the vitality of the brand.

So it will hardly seem strange that one of Cappellini's latest projects is the launch of the Cap-Cafés, which will travel straight from Ho Chi Minh City to Shanghai and Milan. The concept behind the project is to create a space that reflects the spirit of the company, designed from floor to ceiling: from the interiors to the seating, from the tables to the food containers. Even the food—whether eat in or to go, and sold alongside cups and glasses— will clearly reference the world of design and architecture. The pizza for example will not be round but square and come in Mondrian colors.

The various partnerships the firm has kept up over the years demonstrate the fertility of a very free and creative way of understanding brand stretching. The exchanges with artisanal or industrial companies working in different sectors enables the business to share objectives and points of contact and, starting from their different skills, to hybridize each other.

One example is *Paesaggi fluidi*, launched in 2003 as a pioneering project with Philips: a line of hi-tech furnishings combining armchairs and bookcases with consumer electronics such as plasma-screen TV, Hi-Fi or DVD players. In the same spirit projects have been created in co-branding with Radio Tivoli, involving a classic series of radios in different colors and bearing the Cappellini logo. Or with Fiat, which at the launch of its new *500* created a limited edition whose finish and color scheme were designed by Giulio Cappellini. With its blue exterior, elegant moldings and white interiors, the *500 Cappellini* represents his design thinking as it branches out into the world of cars. Other collaborations grew up with the aim of creating customized objects for Cappellini events. In 2011 this led to a special edition bottle by the house of Champagne Pommery produced exclusively for the company.

Cappellini's gaze is alert, curious and attentive to other product sectors. He sees receptiveness not just as brand stretching, but a continuous exercise that enables him to look at himself in a mirror and put himself on the line.

The new *Fiat 500* customized
by Cappellini, presented
at the 2007 Salone del Mobile
in Milan.

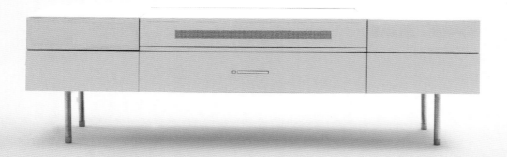

The *Paesaggi Fluidi* project
presented by Cappellini
and Philips at the Salone
del Mobile 2003. *Sideboard*
has a built-in 32" plasma screen:
it disappears into the cabinet
when laid flat.

CASA

HOME

The Real House, exhibition at the Fair for the 2006 Salone del Mobile. Family life inside a glass house fully furnished by Cappellini.

"We have been working in recent years with designers with different approaches and backgrounds to create an international collection of contemporary furniture that epitomizes the idea of living in the nineties," wrote Cappellini in a 1994 catalogue. The same statement is valid today, reflected in his current research into the home: a multicultural dwelling, in which the protagonists are individuals eager to absorb influences from different histories and cultures and live in a setting that represents their identities.

While it is hard to spot a unified hallmark common to all the company's products, a common denominator can be found in their ability to enter **people**'s homes and fit in there. The multiform mingling (formal but also cultural) of the products in its catalogue responds to the complexity of today's homes, where they come to life with the refinement of designer pieces, the ethnic flavor of travel memorabilia and the economic practicality of Ikea furniture. And with the Cappellini catalogue you really could furnish a whole apartment, without sacrificing that variety of styles.

Giulio Cappellini likes to say he is much happier when he sees one of his objects in a house than when he hears it's been added to the permanent collection of a museum. One of his priorities is to respond to the most private desires so that his products can be absorbed into the home.

An idea of the home and the feelings associated with it is expressed in the presentations of products, from installations to communications.

With few exceptions, objects and furnishings are never shown as single designer items but as part of a lived-in setting, helping create an intimate space closely related to the home, the contemporary living space. The urge to recount the concept of the home, not through stereotypes but with great freedom, dominates the way the company has exhibited design over the years, with **exhibitions** and installations focused on the domestic environment.

It began with the house designed in 1992 by Jasper **Morrison** and James Irvine at the Fabbrica del Vapore in Milan, followed by the virtual home with walls traced on the ground with simple white lines, set in an old factory in Cologne in 2001, and the revisitation of the house of Romeo and Juliet in Verona, where the two young people were a modern couple living in a very contemporary setting with a home gym, with the TV set switched on, food scattered over the sofa and a braided rope symbolically let down from the balcony into the courtyard. Then there was the highly original glass round house, with a family living in it for a week, devised for the Salone del Mobile in Milan. The project mimicked Big Brother, voyeuristically presenting to the public the everyday lives of mother, father, two sons and a daughter, proving life can go on quite naturally, even in a designer apartment. One of the latest was finally *Cappellini Home*, assembled in 2012 at the Fondazione Pomodoro, again during Milan Design Week: a hyper-inhabited and hyper-equipped house which played off the most different cultures by mixing together designer products, ethnic items and memorabilia.

Cappellini Home at the
Fondazione Pomodoro during
the 2012 Salone del Mobile:
a sequence of rooms with
Cappellini color scheme
and furniture.

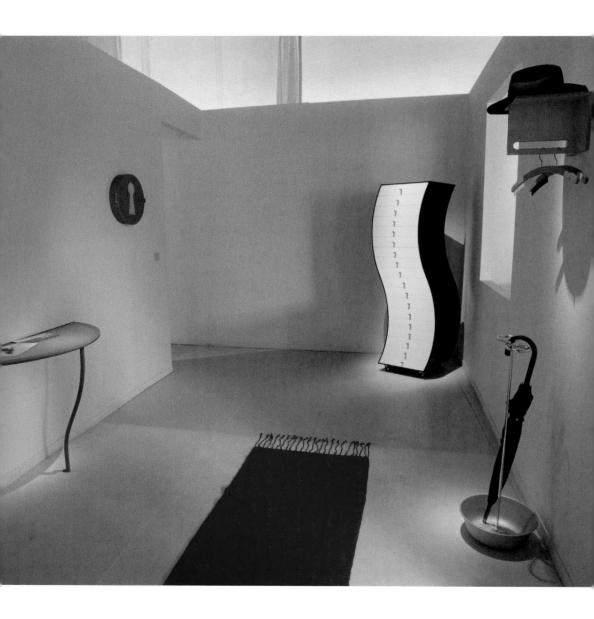

The House of Cappellini,
the setting designed by James
Irvine and Jasper Morrison
at the Fabbrica del Vapore
in 1992.

A casa di Giulietta, curated
by Giulio Cappellini as a fringe
event at Abitare il Tempo,
Verona, 2002.

CASTIGLIONI

T he first retrospective exhibition devoted to Cappellini was *Cappellini: Identities, Analogies, Contradictions Seen by Achille Castiglioni*. It was recounted through three key words that very effectively described the firm's complex and many-sided DNA. The three themes were explored and exhibited for the occasion by the keen and attentive eye of one of the most illustrious names in twentieth-century Italian design.

It was 1996 and the venue was Cologne's Museum für Angewandte Kunst. For the first time in its history it decided to devote an exhibition to a company. The exception implicitly declares the value of what cannot be considered a business in the most commercial sense of the term. Or at least not just a business. As Gabriele Lueg, director of the Museum in Cologne, wrote in the catalogue, the secret lies in Giulio Cappellini's "sure and absolute intuition," noting that the family business "wanted and managed to change; it has devised and continues to devise simple and excellent pieces," but above all "it has discovered young talents who have since became famous and won international recognition." Lueg cites Jasper **Morrison**, Shiro **Kuramata**, Ross Lovegrove, Tom Dixon, Marc **Newson**, James Irvine, Christophe Pillet and Carlo Colombo, all designers present in the exhibition with their analogies and contradictions.

On receiving the invitation to present this exhibition, Cappellini's thoughts immediately turned to Achille Castiglioni, a great architect and the designer of some of the finest exhibit installations ever devised. The mandate was not to think in terms of a classic exhibition, but to look at the company's catalogue and have fun offering a personal interpretation of the works, creating a sort of amusement park. Castiglioni certainly enjoyed himself, stacking and juggling the Cappellini products he selected or using portions of the objects assembled to recount their essence. "The brilliant way Castiglioni 'played' with the exhibits and how he succeeded in grasping their innermost secrets beggars description," commented Lueg. "The master deliberately neglected the commercial aspects; he only presented what he believed to be particularly innovative and expressive. The fact that this exhibition is both visually rich and exciting can be considered a compliment that the master of design made to his younger colleague, and as the affirmation of a design strategy stemming from the avant-garde."

Cappellini recalls the great commitment and professionalism with which Castiglioni devoted himself to this project, from the initial idea to requests for estimates from suppliers and the way he oversaw its whole production, down to the smallest details. "I remember the night before the opening Achille came to check the setup. He saw the lights and didn't

like them, so he asked the workers in charge
to dismantle and reassemble them from scratch.
The technicians were dog tired, but they were so
enthusiastic to be working with a master like him
they unblinkingly redid everything overnight.
In this case, too, Castiglioni showed that to be
great it's not just enough to be creative. You have
to have perseverance and dedication to your
work."

In the texts written for the catalogue
Castiglioni himself recounts his view
of the exhibition. "Designing is all very fine, but
designing well is very demanding. Cappellini's
design *Identities, Analogies, Contradictions*
can be read in his products turned out

in the last ten years in close collaboration with
outstanding designers. The communication
of the characteristics of the designs is highlighted
by the way they are presented in this museum
in Cologne, accentuating and making caricatures
of the projects' complexities and values, together
with a trace of irony. A continuous comparison
between the variability of different design
approaches. In Cappellini a sense of pleasure
for oneself and others is always present. I would
like this exhibition to be remembered not for
a serious, didactic presentation but as a stimulus
to understand that these works are above all
objects that are free and happy when they're
being used and not just contemplated."

Cappellini: Identities, Analogies, Contradictions Seen by Achille Castiglioni (Cologne, 1994).
Photographs of the installation.

The cardboard model created
by Achille Castiglioni for
Cappellini: Identities, Analogies,
Contradictions.

COMPAGNI DI VIAGGIO

TRAVELING COMPANIONS

Ronan Bouroullec, Carlo
Colombo, Erwan Bouroullec,
Jasper Morrison, Giulio
Cappellini and Piero Lissoni
at Superstudio, 2001.

Numbers of designers have crossed the company's path over the past few decades.
With many of them, a first meeting and exchange of ideas with the art director gave rise to projects that eventually became products. With others, there were contacts and long talks, designs and testing of prototypes, but without the product making it into development.

All these people have been traveling companions, an integral part of the Cappellini project.

"Running a company isn't just about turning out products," states Giulio Cappellini. This is why relations with designers take very different forms and have widely varying outcomes. In some cases the firm teams up with a designer to devise an exhibit design, as in the case of **Castiglioni**. In others, the contact involves swapping ideas about possible projects and productions that will never get as far as the catalogue, and this is the case of unfinished or now closed collaborations, yet still important, like those with Konstantin Grcic

or Ross Lovegrove. In yet other cases, designers do a limited edition that goes on sale for a very short period. With some designers the firm does a project that goes beyond the one-off piece, involving other firms or individuals and so creating a broader range of products, as has happened with Irvine and **Morrison**.

Regardless of whether they then joined the **team** or not, Giulio Cappellini still remained on friendly terms with them and kept up a collaboration that proved stimulating to him and the company. "I often meet up these guys that I first met when they were young and they've now become established designers. All have contributed to the company's development, even with a single idea, with a timely word, with a comment on its general philosophy, so that their contribution proved crucial. I still recall some of the hints, ideas or suggestions that maybe at the time did not have any immediate effect on **production** or the firm's general image, but that have somehow influenced the path it took. All have been part of a shared journey and kept us company for part of the way."

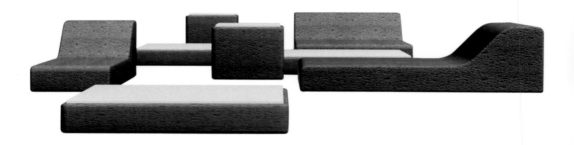

Patricia Urquiola, stone seats
designed for Cappellini.

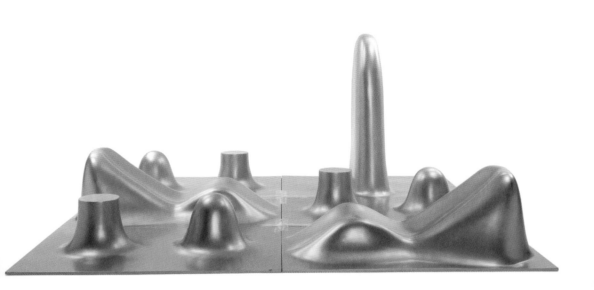

Karim Rashid, seats designed
for Cappellini.

CONCRETEZZA

CONCRETENESS

A new awareness of design: this should be the vocation of the present, according to Giulio Cappellini. After the explosion, in the eighties, of design as a luxury item, a strange object to be acquired in order to enrich the home, an ornament elevated to a status symbol, for some time now things have been changing. Today the **production** of industrial design is moving towards a reinvented simplicity of living, characterized by a spontaneous casualness of harmonies, in the private sector as in contract furnishings or work spaces.

A new concreteness means responding to the functions and needs of everyday life in sustainable ways, but while still setting **people** dreaming.

This is the change from the eighties to the present, visible in the product but also the process. Today designers have a very professional approach. They are no longer people who conceive a "sign," which is then wholly industrialized by the company. Instead they present projects already developed, in the best tradition of Italian Rationalist design, from Vico Magistretti to Carlo Scarpa. Awareness of the designs of these masters seems to be living again in the answers that designers are giving to today's needs. It is no coincidence that Cappellini is rediscovering classics that are still landmarks. "It's crucial to devise serious and restrained projects, reinventing past designs and creating new contemporary classics."

And in this respect, one is reminded of the "small ivory tower," against which **Fronzoni** warned of the need to restore design to the essence of objects. In keeping with the words of the master of minimalism, brought to prominence in the Cappellini catalogue,

1990 advertising campaign.

Orla sofas and armchairs
(2014–2015), Jasper Morrison
for Cappellini.

one has to oppose all that is superfluous and therefore a waste of materials, work, technologies, but also ethical and moral waste.

This approach, which looks at a minimal project understood as a "sincere" relationship between the design and persons, is now reflected in the need to expand the user base, without forsaking creativity. This is no small feat: making a product capable of selling a thousand pieces is much more complicated than designing a sign and selling it to five people.

For a company that has always worked on the large scale, both in terms of quantity (number of objects, installations, events, spaces available) as well as quality, having to come to terms with this new awareness of design means striking a new balance.

The acknowledged genius shown in Giulio Cappellini's foresight and initiative, in the recent years of economic recession has been translated into the ability to stop at the right moment. Although economies and business strategies have changed, his unfailing creativity is always there: gigantism is translated into control, but the secret lies in knowing, even with control, how to reach the same levels.

CONTRADDIZIONI E LIBERTÀ

CONTRADICTIONS AND FREEDOM

Cappellini's presentation at Superstudio during the 2001 Salone del Mobile. Jasper Morrison and Philippe Starck compared.

T o Cappellini freedom means above all freedom of expression, but also freedom for the consumer: the multifaceted identity of the brand, in terms of both style and target, is the culmination of an idea that underlies the all firm's activities and reflects the eclectic tastes of its management. "We're thinking of a new space, a free space, a space that brings together our things, our stories, our contradictions," stated issue number 8 of *CAP*, a magazine containing texts and images that the firm distributed in the nineties. The previous issue, number 7, was dedicated to the theme of "Synthesis" and celebrated the union of different elements into a harmonious, multifaceted whole.

This attraction of opposites was expressed firstly by the variety of products in the Cappellini catalogue, as was rightly pointed out at the exhibition *Identities, Analogies, Contradictions*, curated by Achille **Castiglioni** in Cologne in 1996. The addition of the *Fronzoni '64* line of tables and chairs to the catalogue celebrated the first minimalist piece, while the reissue of the *Proust* armchair by Alessandro Mendini marked the start of a strand of decor coloring products. The freedom of thought declared

in producing these two items at the same time was exemplary and left no room for uncertainty. They decisively marked the harmonious and seductive coexistence of two styles poles apart from each other. And the same conclusions could be drawn from seeing Jasper **Morrison**'s pieces with their sharp lines and the ironic indulgence in softness of Marcel **Wanders**' pieces.

Giulio Cappellini has often been heard to say that "everything and the opposite of everything can coexist," according to those who have worked with him over the last thirty years, adding that his talent has always been the ability to do this harmoniously is integral to his exhibitions as well. Think, for example, of the installation designed for the Milan Fuorisalone at **Superstudio** in 2001. "I called Jasper Morrison and asked him to work on an exhibit design on the floor, telling him the ceiling was white, and at the same time I asked Philippe Starck to think of an installation for the ceiling of the same space, making him believe that the floor would be exposed concrete. When they saw the two things together at first they wanted to kill me, but then they were really happy with the result." It's the story of an impossible collaboration, based on deception, and once again a result of the belief that opposites can coexist in complete freedom.

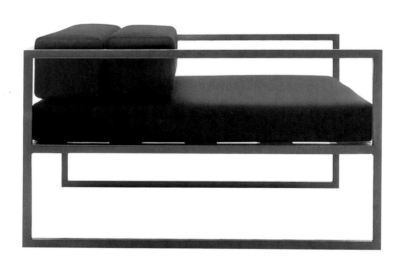

The rigor of the *Fronzoni '64* chair and the irony
of the *Proust* armchair by Alessandro Mendini.
Designed in 1978 and added to the Cappellini
catalogue in 1993, it was presented here in the
Geometric Proust version (2009) with a multicolor
fabric designed by Mendini himself.

DOMENICA

SUNDAY

Giulio Cappellini, *Bong*, lava-stone edition (2015). On the table, a specimen vase by Ronan Bouroullec (1999) and a bottle by Jasper Morrison (1992) from the *Progetto Oggetto* collection.

A
Sunday afternoon designer: this is how Giulio Cappellini describes himself. Though busy running the company, he still hasn't given up his work as designer. It goes back to the early years after he completed his studies together with Rodolfo Dordoni. Together they did projects like the *Aliante* and *Passepartout* bookcases, and then he continued as a solitary designer for both the brand that bears his name and art director at other important firms.

Among the products he designed for Cappellini, many have become pioneers of a way, both rigorous and flexible, of thinking about interiors. An example is the *Sistemi* line, which first introduced a lacquered finish with a broad color palette, as well as making it possible to combine different formats of containers in different compositions.

Other classics are the *Bong* spherical table, the *Luxor* series or the tables *Big Break* and *Gong*.

Under Giulio's guidance, projects with the "Studio Cappellini" signature are also produced. They are developed in-house by a **team** engaged in researching and designing long-selling products, staples of the catalogue and capable of outlasting fashions. The design projects always take second place to the most important project, the company. Cappellini's wry description of himself as a "Sunday afternoon designer" attaches a very personal character to this activity, as if designing is now little more than a hobby and he struggles to find time for it. But, apart from occasional moments devoted to relaxation, communication or interviews, his Sundays are also spent fueling an insatiable curiosity that moves with an interdisciplinary breadth around his passion for design.

FIERE

FAIRS

The Internationale Moebel Messe in Cologne, the Salone del Mobile in Milan, the International Contemporary Furniture Fair in New York, the Paris Design Week or the London version, Abitare il Tempo in Verona and the Biennale Interieur at Kortrijk (Belgium) or the Furniture Fair in Stockholm. There are now any number of industry events and Cappellini has its venue in all of them, while making a selection of its favorite showcases. Depending on the specific case and editions, it may decide to take part directly or organize external events during the fair. Or even just go and have a look around. Among the firm's many appearances, at both national and international level in recent years, there has been a tendency to organize external presentations in Italy, while abroad it prefers to participate internally.

Giulio Cappellini says he has always had a love-hate relationship with trade fairs, perhaps because of their commercial nature. The company's policy is, as far as possible, to put on cultural events rather than commercial displays. In this way fairs become an opportunity to break the mold, identify a theme and look at design from an unexpected standpoint.

This has produced courageous projects like *The Real House* at the Milan fair in 2006, or as the *A casa di Giulietta* as an event during Abitare il Tempo fair in Verona in 2002.

"Every year getting ready for a fair is always a moment of tension. It's almost like taking an examination," admits Giulio. "We try to think of something original, to change and, above all outdo whatever we did the year before. They're immensely important events because within a few days the press and industry specialists get to see a whole year's work. The public see what you've achieved and compare you with other companies. And the feedback of comments and opinions is never so precious as at a fair."

Finally, trade shows are an opportunity to meet other designers, as well as making direct contact with the public. Listening to **people** at first hand is crucial, and all the more so today, when everything can be done at a distance. "In virtual exchanges with designers you can't shake hands, can't get the feel or smell of objects," says Cappellini. "In the midst of the fourth industrial revolution, the digital **innovation**, never forget the human dimension. Even the most sophisticated technology, if not managed by man, can take you so far." Face-to-face meetings offer an opportunity not to forget this.

Milan, the "Cappellini Rooms" installation at the Fair site
for the Salone del Mobile 2013. Deconstructured architectures
form a circular village on two levels, with ten superimposed
boxes displaying different interiors. In the middle of the
floor, all the novelties for 2013 are illuminated by a shower
of *Meltdown* lamps by Swedish designer Johan Lindstén.

The Cappellini stands
at the Salone del Mobile
in Milan: in 2010 (below),
in 2014 (bottom left)
and 2015 (top left): piazzas,
lounge landscapes, domestic
environments and a plurality
of styles.

FRONZONI

AG Fronzoni, chairs in the
Fronzoni '64 series, produced
by Cappellini in 1998.

"**A**im at the essential, eliminate all unnecessary effects, all useless frills, develop a concept on a mathematical basis, around a fundamental idea, a basic structure, stubbornly avoiding waste and excess." In these words AG Fronzoni expressed the principles behind his work. Best known as a great master of graphic design, he is seen by many as the only radically minimalist Italian designer. Cappellini certainly sees him as the only true Italian minimalist in the collection, apart from Claudio Silvestrin, his pupil and direct professional heir (significantly Silvestrin's table *Millenium Hope* (2000) is often displayed together with Fronzoni's table).

Fronzoni described himself as "not an architect, not a graphic designer, not a designer of any kind, but a *projector* capable of solving problems on different scales." Averse to all that is superfluous, not only materially and aesthetically but above all morally, he planned his whole life in terms of the loyalty and spareness of his message. In 1964 he devised a system of tables and chairs, composed on the module of the square, originally designed for his own home. This was a system that could fully furnish a home with geometric rigor and minimalist elegance. Cappellini's **production** of this line of furniture, returned to favor by an exhibition on minimal design curated by Vanni Pasca at Kortrijk in 1995, acknowledged Fronzoni's role in anticipating subsequent events and identified him as a "father" to the young minimalist designers who have always been part of the company's profile.

Reissuing Fronzoni was also an opportunity for Giulio Cappellini to discover the many-sided identity of a fascinating man. "He was not just a rigorous graphic designer, but in his way ironic and a creator of extraordinary objects. A man who was not afraid to change. Of affluent origins, he forced all of his family to abandon a bourgeois lifestyle and live in a **house** from which everything that was superfluous was banished. His story recounts the courage of a choice and how the human soul has many facets, with its coherence and contradictions."

Plain design, stripped of unnecessary decoration, an elementary structure, cheap, no waste of either material or form: these were the key principles of *Fronzoni '64*. The colors could only be black and white, ideally the only ones that represented the rationality of the human mind as opposed to the randomness of nature, the expression of a rigor in the contrast between voids and solids. And Cappellini originally reissued them in black and white, remaining faithful to the absolutism of the theoretical principle that had created them and affirming the total contemporaneity of these boxy, minimalist lines. The bold decision to color Fronzoni came in 2009. Giulio Cappellini decided to produce a variation in the colors of graphics—red, yellow, blue—in a tribute to the profession of their designer. A provocative **innovation** in some respects, introduced with the complicity of Alessandro Mendini, who had been Fronzoni's colleague at the review *Casabella* in 1965 and for five more years. As Mendini wrote in the pages of *Abitare* in 2009 (No. 494), the transformation into color of the 1964 series of furniture entailed a strong scholarly and cultural reflection: "I personally approve this attitude, which gives a 'Second Life' to our great friend and master AG Fronzoni. But the question may give rise to discordant opinions and even objections. Many of Fronzoni's fans might well disagree an call it sacrilege. Rummaging in my memory, I recall that Fronzoni gave permission for color images in *Casabella*, provided they were monochromatic and consisted of the basic colors in the four-color process, namely red, yellow and blue (see the covers of numbers 321 and 322). In this respect, Giulio Cappellini's operation is coherent with Fronzoni's approach to colors, and all the more so when he speaks of him as a graphic artist rather than a designer. Moreover, artists highly appreciated by Fronzoni were Theo van Doesburg (plastic architecture), Jean Gorin (Groupe Espace), Gerrit Rietveld, Georges Vantongerloo and generally the De Stijl group, with 'graphic architecture' characterized by its color. What then? We will leave open

the whole question of *Fronzoni '64* in colors, listing some potential areas for discussion:
1. Is it the natural extension of a project already implicit in the author's method and intentions?
2. Or is it a careful redesign, a re-invention due to Cappellini, of a narrative interpretation?
3. Is it a choice that tends to update a product that is too Calvinistic when viewed in black and white and to guide it towards new trends?
4. Is it a refinement that contradicts Fronzoni's harsh and rigid method?
5. Is it a generous desire to bring an important master too long overlooked to the fore?
Five interesting questions to ponder.
It is certain that Giulio Cappellini, who worked so much on minimalism in his catalogue, could not fail to retrace its Italian origins and propose its most precise symbol, namely AG Fronzoni. And Cappellini, this very able discoverer and rediscoverer of talent, perhaps wanted, with these three 'basic' colors, to display that 'basic' sweetness of soul of this master of Bottega Grafica, which has remained hidden."

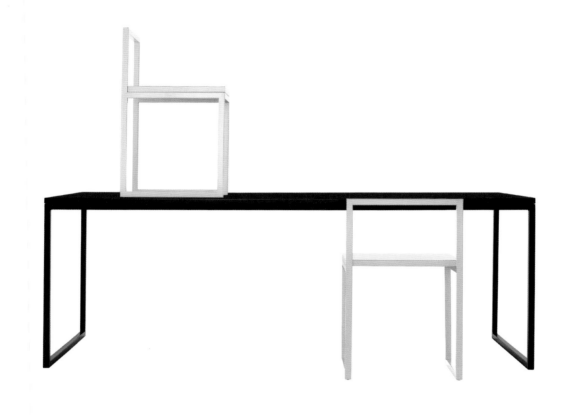

Fronzoni '64 in color.
The edition presented in 2009
replaced austere black and
white with the colors of printers
graphics: yellow, red and blue.

Marking the fiftieth anniversary of the *Fronzoni '64* series in 2014,
at the Ristorante Carlo e Camilla in Segheria in Milan, Cappellini
presented the *50th Anniversary Edition*: a limited series in two-
tone white/black or black/white, and a new version of the table,
based on sketches in AG Fronzoni's archive, with a stainless steel
frame and two variant tops in either Carrara marble or ash.

IDENTITÀ, PENSIERO E IRONIA

IDENTITY, THOUGHT AND IRONY

Cappellini Corporate Image, 2015.

"**C**appellini rests on a cultural rather than a business project. We want to sell not just products but contents in general. I believe that companies can be divided into good producers and points of reference. We hope to be a point of reference. To make a mark it's not enough just to make beautiful chairs, you have to have a comprehensive project. The products need not necessarily to be beautiful, but the clarity of the company's project is essential. This has to be the starting point."

An idea, clear and immediate, that does not require many words. This is the indispensable condition for Giulio Cappellini's every idea. Because, as Carlo Scarpa said, if we have to spend a lot of words talking about a project it means we are not certain of it in the first place. And the most important project need not to be that of a single product: neither **Morrison**'s *Thinking Man Chair* nor Dixon's *S Chair*, nor any other object in the collection that has become an icon. It is that firm's ensemble, conceived in the round: a multi-faceted project, but which has a clearly defined thread running through it and holding together the different pieces. An idea capable of reinventing itself and responding to the diversity of times and places, but instantly recognizable in all its facets.

"There is great consistency in the projects we present. There's a common thread that governs every phase and every aspect of them, ranging from the product to its presentation, from the event to the invitation, from the display to the catalogue." Andrea Castelli, who has worked for the company since 2000, recounts: "The initial input made by Giulio, the color, the forms given to space, also guide communication in the same way. The company's work is made up of many pieces of a huge puzzle forming a coherent whole." And in putting together the pieces of the puzzle, the sense of unity emerges ever more clearly, and the idea is presented in its immediacy. Usually the identity of the communication project starts from the concept devised in Milan and is then dragged around the world for the rest of the year with continuous adaptations and reinventions. The *idea* is developed internally but through comparison with other disciplines (fashion, architecture, art) and with partners and suppliers who work with the company. They are not only responsible for carrying out the more

Fabio Novembre, *Org* (2001).

technical roles, but participants in the group project, making their contribution in terms of ideas and **innovation**.

The creation of beautiful objects and captivating products arises through ideas and exchanges. And even the latent problems brought to light by the crisis should not mean giving up coherent thinking and creativity, with the aim of designing, producing and presenting products that are not gestures as an end in themselves but capable of entering **people**'s homes and memories and enduring in time.

With the clarity of this idea, Cappellini works on a catalogue that is never tedious or excessively way out, but has its own lively lightness, with contradictions and fractures within it that match the variety of styles and trends of the contemporary world.

Then a significant aspect of Cappellini's identity is a certain irony. The ability to mix very different styles, with great lightness and freedom, is in itself

a sign of a sense of humor that is found in its products, displays and visual identity.

Cappellini is hardly a company dedicated to minimalism, although it discovered Jasper Morrison, has reissued the furniture series designed by **Fronzoni**, pursued and finally produced the objects designed by Shiro **Kuramata**. Proving that the facets of the prism are endless and "everything and the opposite of everything can coexist," alongside this strand there is a great deal more. There are Tom Dixon, Marc **Newson**, Fabio Novembre, and Mendini's *Proust* armchair. There is the revival of a Pop taste, rounded shapes, characters that make products more like toys and represent an ironic approach to design.

The same vital and dynamic approach is found in its communication projects, with a range of different messages capable of regaling people with happiness and eliciting a smile. And they help the firm not to take itself too seriously.

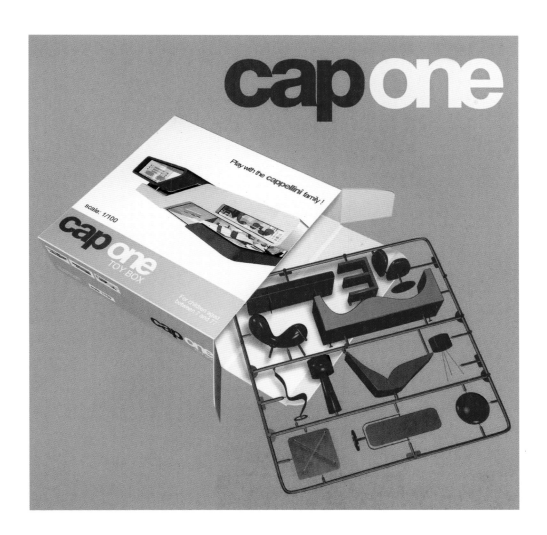

CD *Cap One* with publication
and scale models of some
Cappellini products (design
by Nuphonic – Ora Ito, 2002).

INNOVAZIONE

INNOVATION

"For me the real innovation today is to make extraordinarily normal products, not hyped but with a high aesthetic, functional and technological content. It means being contemporary and attentive to the evolution of design: not just creating new forms, but working on new materials, sustainable if possible, never tested on production techniques and unusual textures, also drawing from other sectors. So you can create objects that are friendlier and, if possible, more accessible to the general public. Being innovative is still quite complex: it is a drive that has to be part of the firm's DNA, not just a marketing tool."

If these are the premises, there is no doubt that in Cappellini the urge for innovation remains in its DNA, today as in the past. Innovation is not only technical, typological or stylistic, determining the choice and development of products, but also linked to the idea that governs the larger scheme of the company and reflects its leader's vision.

There is never the rigidity of an unequivocal and inviolable idea in every project undertaken, whether it is product, communication or display. The process is a continuous work in progress and every phase is assessed in complete freedom until the best solution emerges.

A project presented the month before remains in continuous evolution, up to the minute before the trade fair opens or **production** starts. Everything that was decided around a table in most cases proves to be different from what is eventually produced, because it is only in the **concreteness** of fabrication that feelings reveal which is the correct solution.

The only factor likely to cramp the company's work is economic, especially in the recent recession years. Innovation is translated into a careful response to its time, in seeking an immediate result, but this does not mean it is solely commercial or less creative. Cappellini is a firm willing to take risks, accept challenges, go for a gamble. The challenge today also lies in identifying new production systems, with the rationality and practicality that guided the work of the great masters in the fifties.

One of the most recent projects launched by Cappellini is the maximum expression of the company's urge (and need) to be always

Presented at "Cappellini Next" in 2015, the *Embroidery Chair*
by Swedish designer Johan Lindstén reinterprets the ancient
technique of embroidery, using technology to take it to an advanced
aesthetic level in tune with the present.

Opposite: *Trez* armchair by the Brazilian designer Zanini de Zanine: presented at "Cappellini Next" in 2012, it went into production the following year in white, red and black versions.

Stool in the *Mutation* series by Maarten de Ceulaer, also presented by "Cappellini Next" 2015. hand-crafted by the designer, it seems to have grown organically by cell mutation.

active and innovative, reflecting its searching, exploratory spirit. This is "Cappellini Next," the flagship of its official collection presented for the first time at the 2012 Salone del Mobile in Milan and repeated annually. It is a collection in progress, which previews the objects that could potentially go into production the following year, as they were originally conceived by the designers, before being re-engineered by the firm. Hence it is the designers themselves who lavish care on every detail, ranging from design to fabrication, in complete freedom and without any commercial pressure to compromise. This choice rewards **manual skills** and **multiculturalism**, with a selection of designers from all latitudes, giving prominence to the cultural backgrounds and craft traditions of their respective countries. "Cappellini Next" embodies not just great innovation but also a strong entrepreneurial spirit. It identifies the designers and makes them its own, getting them to entrust it with the prototypes for a year to assess their feasibility, while showing that the firm is always on the move, it is present and looks ahead, already knowing what the coming trend is going to be.

KURAMATA

I t all started over a sushi lunch, a date fixed laboriously. The meeting with Shiro Kuramata was one of the most important for Giulio Cappellini and the company, which made him its poster boy in presenting themselves on the international stage.

It was 1985 and, on his first trip to Japan, Giulio Cappellini had seen some of Kuramata's one-off pieces in a gallery. He had promised himself that, one day, he would produce those objects. Back in Italy, through their mutual friend Ettore Sottsass, he managed to get in touch with him. "I got Shiro's telex number from him and started to write. For a month I received no answer, though I was very insistent. At Ettore's suggestion I decided to start sending him private letters, looking for a more personal means of communication that would give me the certainty of reaching him directly. One day I received a letter from Kuramata in which he wrote: 'Dear Mr Cappellini, I am very happy because today the almond trees are in bloom.' I didn't lose a moment. I got straight on a plane to Japan."

In their long meeting, eating sushi and trying to understand each other (Kuramata expressed himself only in Japanese), Giulio Cappellini won the chance to produce objects that would soon become part of the company's catalogue. After the great designer's early death in 1991, when he was just 56 years old, Cappellini and the foundation bearing Kuramata's name

continued to reissue his pieces and conduct scholarly research into the artist/designer's many projects.

"The aspects that appeal to me in Shiro Kuramata's designs are their poetry, lightness and irony. His objects are extraordinarily innovative and curious, never banal. They are useful and above all capable of setting us dreaming." Cappellini describes Kuramata as a thoughtful man of great culture, who paid close attention to **people** and wished to be considered not as a number in the mass but as a distinctive personality. He was a man inspired by art, with great respect and admiration for the masters, to whom his "homages" bore testimony. One of the most important Japanese designers to date, Kuramata is an expression of that "poetic essentialism" that has come to characterize design in his land. In the course of his career he was the creator of a series of pieces that were eventually recognized as landmarks in the history of twentieth century design.

There is no doubt that the presentation of his products in 1986 was a great cultural breakthrough for Cappellini. It marked the transition from a furniture manufacturer to a leader in the evolution of contemporary design worldwide. The projects that entered the catalogue over the years are many and all have their own poetic touch: the *Bookshelf* bookcase, with its compartments of different sizes from one another, perfectly punctuates spaces with natural light. The chests of drawers in the *Progetti compiuti* collection playfully define

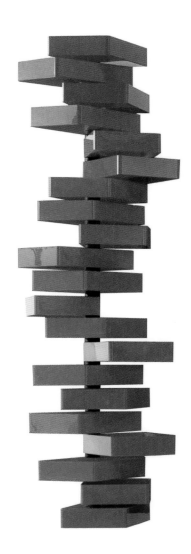

Shiro Kuramata, *Revolving Cabinet* (1970).

Shiro Kuramata, *Solaris* (1977). The cabinet belongs to the *Progetti compiuti* range, returned to production by Cappellini in 1985. Its elongated legs, in natural aluminum colored metal, support the body that seems to float, with drawers in black-stained ash and knobs in black lacquered metal. On the right the sketch *Homage to Andrei Tarkovsky*, the filmmaker who inspired and gave his name to the object: both are the product of the subconscious and a layering of memories.

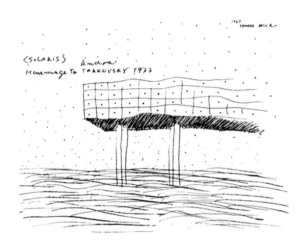

the setting in which they are placed by their volumes and the mystery of some drawers easily accessible and others in which to keep one's secrets. *Dinah* is like a totem in the landscape of the home, with its eighteen drawers set one above the other and opening on both sides. *Revolving Cabinet*, consisting of twenty drawers stacked and rotating around a vertical metal support. It has a colored form that can change at our pleasure. *Pyramid* is an enigmatic interplay of transparencies and solid volumes. *Homage to Mondrian* is hybridized with art in a way typical of Shiro Kuramata. *Ko-Ko* is the epitome of the essence of a seat.

In addition to items what went into production, Cappellini has devoted two important **exhibitions** to Kuramata. The first was the *Progetti compiuti* series, the one that inaugurated the designer's collaboration with the company, presented at the Museo di Milano in 1986. The second, presented since 2010 at various venues, was *Homage to Shiro*, which exhibited not only the iconic products that are still part of the Cappellini catalogue, but also reproductions of original drawings and prototypes. A tribute to the man and the designer that indelibly marked Cappellini and his company. "A few months before he died, I spent a whole afternoon with him in his studio in Tokyo, almost without uttering a word. He was working on projects, playing with pieces of colored plexiglass, which changed brightness and color depending on the movements of the sun. Shiro taught me that frequently long silences are worth more than many words."

Chests of drawers on wheels *Side 1* and *Side 2*, designed by
Kuramata in 1970: the sinuous forms make up two different variants
of drawers lacquered white, stacked high and enclosed in a black ash
wood frame. To the left, image from the 1986 advertising campaign,
with *Side 2* communicating with a traditional setting and the
Callimaco lamp designed by Ettore Sottsass for Artemide in 1982.
Above, the furniture in the display at the *Progetti compiuti* exhibition
in the Museo di Milano (1986).

LIMITED EDITION

T he most iconic products in the Cappellini collection over the years have often been reinterpreted and offered to the public in limited editions. These are series of just a few items that make no claim to be works of art, but are rather meant as revisitations, often ironic, of certain projects that have shaped the history of the company's catalogue.

In this way, Tom Dixon's *S Chair* has been turned into *Bolide*, in a stretched version like a chaise longue. Or, again, it assimilates a texture that presents the Cappellini brand name exploded, with the letters running across a white or black base, like the ones presented in a number of advertising campaigns that urged the public to investigate space "in all its definitions."

Then Marcel **Wanders'** *Knotted Chair* has undergone various mutations: the chrome plating of *Knotted Future*, introduced in 2001, made the chair look metallic, then it was colored red in *Knotted Rouge*. Another star of the limited edition, Wanders' lamp *Big Shadow*, has been repeatedly transformed with the introduction of textures with bright colors, so changing it from an all-white light source into a furnishing with a highly decorative character. Or again a great classic like Jasper **Morrison'**s *Thinking Man's Chair* has been issued in limited editions with new and different colors.

These interpretations are consistent with the spirit of a company that likes to innovate continuously, never standing still or letting the public get used to its image, which remains true to itself. They are not meant as celebrations, but reinterpretations. They offer different ways of seeing products that are now well known but whose creativity still offer many facets to be explored, in a spirit that is often closer to the vision of the art world.

Marcel Wanders, *Knotted Future* and *Knotted Rouge*, 2001.

S Chair, Cappellini limited
edition, 2003.

Marcel Wanders, limited
edition of *Big Shadow*
in printed silk and gold (2005)
and *Eye Shadow* (2013).

LISSONI

Piero Lissoni, sideboard, desk and table from the *Lochness* range (2015).

P iero Lissoni and Giulio Cappellini grew up together. They both attended the Faculty of Architecture at the Milan Polytechnic, though in different years, and both hail from Brianza. The relation between the two is based on close friendship, on holidays spent together, many shared moments and trust won over time. "Working with Piero proves that you can work with friends. It's not true that friends can't say things openly or create good projects," says Giulio. Today they often find themselves sharing not just projects, readings and presentations, which they start by talking about design and end up remembering anecdotes of when they were boys. The balance of their partnership is based on the different ways they think about design and the contrasts between their characters, with Cappellini's exuberance tempered by Lissoni's discretion.

"Piero is someone who likes to see his products manufactured in absolutely neutral colors: blacks, greys, whites, and beiges. I often tease him by turning out prototypes in the strong colors of our catalogue. We thrash these ideas out and argue about them at length, always getting good results."

Lissoni has spent his whole professional life pursuing a simple and elegant approach, in product design as in graphics or architecture. The furnishings he has devised for the Cappellini marque reveal a formal rigor that is never banal and a concern for balanced, simple lines. His sensibility reflects one of the firm's two sides, the one devoted to minimalist, highly contemporary design.

This is shown by the first series of projects such as the *Soft* sofas (1996), then articulated in the *Supersoft* armchair (1998) and the *Crossoft* chair (2005), as well as more recent developments, like the *Lochness* family of products (2015), which includes a sideboard with two doors, a series of containers, tables and a desk with drawers and a drawer pedestal. But Lissoni's rigor encounters Cappellini's sensibility with a touch of irony, as in the limited series of the classic *330* seat, sheathed in 2013 with a plain hand-painted linen cover with a fruit and flower pattern and an inscription that is a manifesto to Italy: "Viva l'Italia."

UNI container by Piero Lissoni,
in HDF with double doors in
poplar plywood combined with
aluminum and wooden drawers
(2000).

The lacquered container from
the *Lochness* range by Piero
Lissoni, with single door
and removable tray (2014).

MANUALITÀ DEL FARE

MANUAL SKILLS IN THE MAKING

A chille **Castiglioni** said "first you make the products and then design them." Giulio Cappellini sees this statement as the basis of the whole process. Design is a practical matter, it means getting your hands dirty. It is crucial to immerse yourself in the various stages of design, then find the right synergies with technology. "When it comes to visualizing, there's no doubt that the computer marked a big step forward. But renderings, however beautiful, lack concreteness in the details and practicality. Technology is fine provided it doesn't deprive a design of its truth factor."

Every project has two sides: ideation, which includes conception and formal composition, and prototyping. These two phases are complementary. They often go together synchronously, proceeding by trial and error and entailing the essential coexistence of manual skill and technology. In the catalogue of Cappellini products, the two processes often persist into **production**, with highly industrialized phases alternating with others requiring the human touch and handiwork. Projects such as *Low Pad* by Jasper **Morrison** or *Rainbow*

Chair by Patrick **Norguet** are clear examples of the encounter between technology and craftsmanship, in a process that can be termed **post-industrial**.

The firm's engineering of the projects submitted by designers is based on their production, sometimes in large numbers. It does not exclude the artisanal component. Rather it is the necessary condition for identifying the correct strategies and subsequently achieving the best result in the product.

Great stress is also laid on the creation by designers of their projects at an earlier stage, before prototyping by the firm. The "Cappellini Next" program, by presenting to the public a sample physically created by individual designers, relates this propensity to enhance the manual quality of making. In addition to being a tangible sign of **innovation** and a gaze towards the future, it enhances the concreteness of a process developed by designers of different nationalities, who work with a variety of craft techniques related to their own backgrounds. The urge to analyze how the thought of contemporary design moves in different countries while promoting local manufactures thus leads to a selection that is a clear expression of the geographical

Producing the *Prehistoric Aliens* tables by Glimpt Studio ("Cappellini Next," 2013) the outcome of a period spent working in craft workshops in Peru.

Meltdown lamp by Johan Lindstén (2013 for *Progetto Oggetto*) and phases of fabrication.

and cultural influences of the designers' origins. By bringing together ideas and craftsmanship, designers create objects made using materials and techniques from various parts of the world, from Brazil to France, India, Norway, the Czech Republic and the United States. The Brazilian Zanini de Zanine designed a chair inspired by the plastic arts of his country and made with the same metal used for the roofs of the favelas. The Indians Sahil&Sarthak used the oddments left over from carpet-making, a local product, to make a multicolored armchair. In Eastern Europe Jan Plechac twisted wire to create an armchair out of an interlacing pattern of circles.

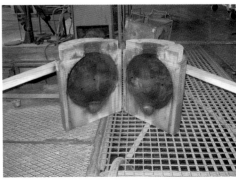

Projects presented at "Cappellini Next" 2012: *Circle Armchair*
by Jan Plehac & Henry Wielgus, *Stork Chairs* by Sahil&Sarthak,
Trez by Studio Zanini, *Dancing Chair* by Constance Guisset
and *Daddy Longlegs* stools by Martin Solem.

MATERIA

MATTER

Bakery Studio, *NOM Nature of Material*, presented at the 2010 Salone del Mobile in Milan and produced by Cappellini in 2012. A detail of the stool made from a folded sheet of aluminum perforated by laser.

"**A**ll materials, no matter if they are natural or artificial, have specific properties that are necessary to understand in order to know how to use them. New materials, as well as new building systems, do not guarantee superiority on their own. The correct relationship between them is crucial. Each material is only worth that which we are able to obtain from it." With these words, Mies van der Rohe expressed his ideas about the need to relate to techniques and tools. The quote is very dear to Giulio Cappellini, who uses it to back up his conviction of the importance of starting not from a product but a material and trying to enhance its properties.

In this experiment several designers who work with Cappellini are to the fore, sharing a common passion in this respect. To quote one of the most representative and recent cases, think of the *NOM* (*Nature of Material*) series by the Israeli couple Bakery Studio. Starting with the idea of reproducing the folds of origami in a sheet of aluminum folded and perforated by laser, Ran Amitai and Gilli Kuchik designed a collection of stackable tables that are given their final form in a bending mold. The designers manipulate and work with the material. Ran Amitai guides the form, with a very traditional hands-on approach.

The company's internal research team, at the urging of its art director, also tests materials and unusual finishes and passes on ideas to designers. These ventures often break new ground and kindle new passions, as happened in with upholstered furniture and glued fabric (eliminating the seams) or laminates. Or they put forward bewildering ideas by presenting icons revisited in their design and transformed by the use of different materials. These ideas are always guided by the interplay of contrasts, in the freedom of juxtapositions and interpretations.

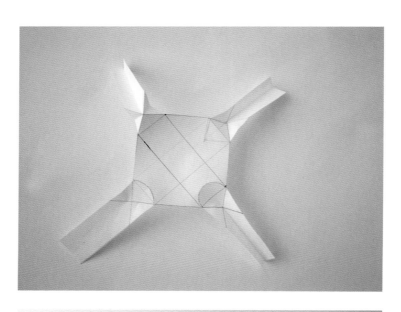

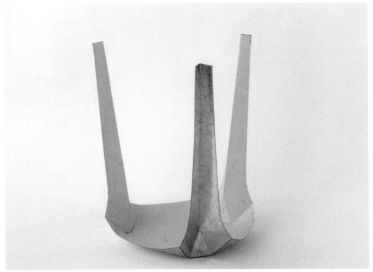

Study models of the *NOM*
stool, from paper to aluminum
sheet, reproducing origami
folds.

MONDO E MULTICULTURALITÀ

WORLD AND MULTICULTURALISM

With his inquiring mind, Giulio Cappellini began to travel soon after taking over the company, seeking to understand what was happening in the world in terms of creativity. This was not because he underrated the local know-how, but he felt the need for an international openness that would lead Italian companies to work with young designers from abroad, so expanding its scope.

At the start of the eighties, well aware of the debt Italian design owed to the extraordinary partnerships between young designers, such as Gio Ponti, Gae Aulenti, Marco Zanuso, Achille **Castiglioni** and Ettore Sottsass, and a series of enlightened entrepreneurs who created a new form of business, he promoted that international openness that was the natural evolution of the fashion for Italian products. It was marked initially by a selection of young European talents and then extended to the whole world, interpreting a sensibility that today places the same emphasis on craftsmanship as on new technologies.

"Cappellini Love" is a project that, in recent years, has expressed the company's ambition to work not only with designers from around the world, but also to engage with the most remote craft traditions normally used only to make traditional products that rarely travel beyond the borders of their own countries. By getting young European designers to work in countries ranging from Africa to the Far East, Cappellini created partnerships with the Nelson Mandela Foundation (which flowed into the handmade tables made from recycled paper designed by Stephen Burks) or the Peruvian cooperative Artesanos Don Bosco, which cherishes local crafts and creates employment opportunities in the most isolated villages of the Andes (where the Swedish designers Glimpt Studio have been working in local workshops producing a series of more modern furnishings, the *Prehistoric Aliens* coffee tables). Glimpt Studio also produced the *Superheroes* series of chairs, the result of a trip to Vietnam during which Mattias Rask and Tor Palm visited several workshops to study their techniques, materials and colors. "Cappellini Love" is the expression of a quest that goes beyond the clichés of ethnic fashions to enter a horizon of **innovation** and at the same time foster local traditions.

Above: The factory sheds of the Fabbrica del Vapore, the venue
for the presentation of "Mondo" in 1992 as part of the Cappellini
event for the Salone del Mobile.

Below: "Mondo" corporate image, 1988.

Presentation of "Mondo"
at the Cappellini showroom
at Carugo in 1991.

A forerunner of this trend, however,
was the "Mondo" (World) project, launched
in 1987 by a collaboration between Giulio
Cappellini and Paola Navone. At the time it gave
a strong boost to Milanese design. It was the start,
a search that threw open doors to craft skills from
around the planet. Established as an independent
company, it has since become a Cappellini
brand. The first collection was called *Dejavu* and
was a contemporary reinterpretation of the classic
wicker products of the Far East. Then there
was the collection *Mondo Notte*, with a series
of wrought-iron objects, and *Mondo Cina,* inspired
by ancient Chinese furniture with a modern twist.

"A very strong project in terms of both
product and communication, which proved
highly successful not only critically but also
commercially. While Cappellini is decidedly
more a niche product, "Mondo" was more
transversal and appealed to design buffs,
to affluent ladies as well as young radicals,"
Giulio Cappellini observes looking back.
The company continues to promote the project
as a way of listening to a contemporary world
in which the most sophisticated design adorns
homes together with relics of travel and where
the boundaries between countries tend to be ever
less clearly marked.

Glimpt Studio, *Superheroes*
for "Cappellini Love," in the
catalogue since 2012. Stages
in the fabrication of the
stools, inspired by a trip
to Vietnam and observation
of customs, craft techniques,
local materials and colors.

MORRISON

H
—

is encounter with Jasper Morrison was one of Giulio Cappellini's first and most important meetings. It was 1987 and in London Zeev Aram was celebrating the twenty-third anniversary of the opening of his **showroom** with an exhibition devoted to the best ideas and innovations of the country's recent graduates. The exhibits included the prototype of the *Thinking Man's Chair* which Jasper Morrison, just out of the Royal College of Art, had designed the previous year for a trade show in Japan. The chair immediately clicked with Cappellini, the first producer to express an interest in the young British designer, who soon became well known and successful. In the days before email and cell phones, making contact meant going to an address provided by the college. "So I dropped in at Jasper's home-studio-workshop and told him I had seen his prototype and wanted to produce it. I remember he stood gazing at me in astonishment, drinking a glass of water and saying nothing. I suggested he should come to Milan and offered him a plane ticket for the following day." The next day was too soon,

but a date was fixed for the following week. So, over a dish of pasta, a partnership was formed that has continued for almost thirty years, leading not just to a number of objects becoming long sellers but also a sharing of ideas and larger-scale projects. "In our meetings we end up talking an hour about his designs and three hours about the company. Jasper has had and continues to have a vital role. Working with him is a great experience, where you think of the product but also general strategies, leaving nothing to chance."

Presented at the Salone del Mobile in Milan in 1988, the *Thinking Man's Chair* was Morrison's first great success and Cappellini's opening move on the international stage. The idea of creating a chair consisting only of its structural elements was inspired by an old chair lacking an upholstered seat, glimpsed outside a store. The final project assembles the tubular metal of the frame and the flat profiled seat and back, with two flat glass-holders at the ends of the armrests. Initially it was to be called the *Drinking Man's Chair*, but ended up with a more sophisticated name, inspired by the slogan on a packet of wire pipe cleaners used to assemble the model. The radius of curvature handwritten on the individual pieces

Invitation designed by Jasper Morrison for the exhibition
at the Spazio Romeo Gigli, Salone del Mobile, 1989.

Following pages: the installation curated by Morrison himself
with the console *One-Legged Table* and *Day Bed* presented that year,
in addition to *Thinking Man's Chair.*

of the metal structure, as was done for the first prototype, is the only decoration on a chair which rejects all ornament.

In the late eighties and early nineties, Morrison took part in the firm's activities not only by putting forward his products, but also by curating some important presentations. He also launched the idea, together with his friend James Irvine, for a broader collective project for home accessories, which was then embodied in the **Progetto Oggetto** collection inaugurated in 1992.

The exhibition organized in Milan during the 1999 Salone del Mobile sealed Morrison's eleven years of collaboration with the company with a great success.

It launched a series of products on which they had been working together for some time, seeking to strike the perfect balance between formal result, technical solution and quality **production**. Displayed on transparent boxes filled with flowers, there appeared for the first time pieces destined to last many years: the *Hi Pad* and *Low Pad* chairs, the *Elan* sofa, the *Sleeper* bed, the *Gamma* table and the *Plan* container system. These projects were then followed by other great successes like the *Tate* (2000), *Lotus* (2006), and *Bac* (2009) chairs, the *Morrison Stools* (2003), the collection of *Gambetta* (2012) upholstered furniture, and the *Superoblong* (2004) sofas, later rethought based on a seamless modular system in *Oblong* (2013).

An example of the perfect functional, technical and aesthetic synthesis produced by the partnership between Cappellini and Morrison is the fabrication of the *Low Pad* and *Hi Pad* chairs. Inspired by the spareness and elegance of the chairs by the Danish designer Poul Kjaerholm, they were designed to secure the maximum reduction in volume with greater comfort. After the first prototypes, based on a conventional fabric covering, research devised a way of modeling the fabric or leather directly on the mold, with a technology similar to that used for automobile seats. This led to the final system, with a plywood core of beech covered with polyurethane foam of different thicknesses sliced by CNC machines.

Assembly is partly manual. The wooden structure is glued to the foam padding on the seat and back, to which the coating of fabric or leather is then applied with hand pressure, so as to follow the shape of the foam blocks. The result, thanks to Morrison's design skills and Capppellini's technical expertise with upholstery, was an example of meticulous joint research.

The prototypes were repeated to check and refine every detail, in a continuous exchange of ideas that left no room for mistakes. Perhaps this great rigor is the secret of these starkly elegant products, which place function before expression. And that acquire ever greater value with the passing of time.

MOSTRE

EXHIBITIONS

C ontamination, disorientation, excitement: these are keywords driving displays of Cappellini products. We could add to them: **home**, play, poetry, irony. Whether it's at a trade **fair** or in a store, a **showroom** or an event, Giulio Cappellini is not content to make simple presentations of objects ranged side by side. He prefers to transcend retailing and focus on feelings, seeking for modes, codes and places not normally used for this purpose and in this sector.

The challenges that have brought the company its reputation, by devising new languages and new fashions, concern not just international openness or wagering on unknown names, but also the ways it displays design.

Among the first projects that reflected this orientation were the veritable exhibitions organized at the Museo di Milano in Via Sant'Andrea, with an installation designed together by Rodolfo Dordoni and Patrizia Scarzella: *La stanza si mette in mostra* (1985), *Out of scale. Mobili Maiuscoli* (1987), and above all *Progetti compiuti*, in 1986, celebrating the start of **production** of the series of objects of the same name, perhaps the most

important collection by the great Japanese designer Shiro **Kuramata**. This exhibition has become an important part of the history of design, almost as significant as the products it celebrated. The objects, displayed on daises, were immersed in clouds of smoke, in a penumbra evoking a mystical dimension. The visitor was led by "light paths" marked by lasers from room to room, in an utterly contemporary and unexpected mode of display.

Those who worked for Cappellini also recall the displays at Carugo, in the original company headquarters. "During the Salone del Mobile in Milan, as well as other times, we used to organize events that placed this little town in Brianza, with no more than 4,000 inhabitants, at the center of the international paths of design. They were truly festive occasions and everyone used to talk about them. In this respect we were almost the forerunners of fashion parties, transcending the furniture sector in ways that were completely unknown at Carugo (and elsewhere)." The streets would be lit with candlelight leading to the venue in Via Cavour. The forgotten province would be awakened by the vision of a man who knew the world and conceived displays for Carugo as if it was Milan

Exhibition at Harrods
department store, London.

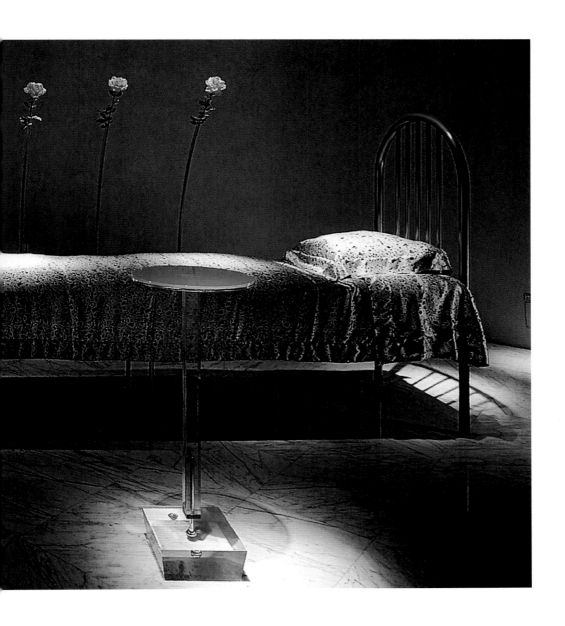

Shiro Kuramata for "Cappellini
Arte," April 1991.

or New York. "This feeling is perhaps a result of Giulio's origins. He was born and raised in Brianza and is attentive to the little things, the values of hidden places and ordinary lives, in contrast with the greatness of his gifts and the things he has achieved."

Into his installations flow ideas and stimuli absorbed while traveling, as well as a passion for contemporary art and other fields, reinvented and transposed into design ideas conceived by a man with his gaze projected forward, to whom whatever has just been devised already seems obsolete. Whenever certain methods of display become somehow recognized, he immediately feels he has to change course. In the first group exhibition on Cappellini, designed in 1996 by Achille **Castiglioni** at the museum in Cologne, the brief was not make a museum exhibition but to imagine the Cappellini products as if they were in funfair. Hence the rule is once again to play on opposition and disorientation by devising codes and languages capable of surprising.

The exhibition at Romeo and Juliet's **house** in Verona in 2002, on the occasion of Abitare il Tempo, also played on a contrast, in this case between past and future. "Having the opportunity to work in a historical place added a charm that could not be found in other installations. We devised the layout room by room, seeking to create a contact between the historic house and a very contemporary decor. What you felt, and it was fun to imagine, was the way literary figures of the past like Romeo and Juliet

would have lived amid Cappellini furniture," says Andrea Castelli, who has been in charge of Cappellini's exhibit designs since 2000.

The most important exhibition internationally focused on the recovery of an abandoned factory—another topic very dear to Giulio Cappellini—formerly used to manufacture diesel engines. The space was laid out on four levels around a large central light well which in 2001 hosted Cappellini's participation in the Cologne trade fair. In such an immense complex Cappellini's idea of the home had to be reworked into a project capable of filling the spaces. The goal was to create numbers of displays, each different from the others, that would generate curiosity in the route running through the four floors. From the top, overlooking the central atrium, it opened out onto the most amazing sight: a home with virtual walls traced with white marks on the paintings suspended in the void and the furnishings arranged in the rooms. Besides the many **exhibitions** designed in **showrooms** and at trade fairs around the world, and those that marked the birth and growth of new districts and key locations of the Fuorisalone in Milan, in more recent years two modular exhibits, smaller and easily transportable, have traveled to various locations. They are *Homage to Shiro* and *Cappellini's Heroes*, two "professions of love" to the designers who have shaped the company's history. While the former was obviously a tribute to the great Japanese designer, the second was a kind of anthology of products that have become icons of the company's identity.

Cappellini exhibition at the Salone del Mobile in Milan (2005),
at the Palazzo delle Ex Poste on Via Ferrante Aporti, partly
redeveloped for the occasion. The year's new designs and some great
classics are set in a monochrome ambiance set off by the lighting
and perspective.

Following pages: Cappellini window display at Harrods in London.

NENDO

Nendo, ten years
of collaboration with
Giulio Cappellini. Sketch
for the exhibition devoted
to the Japanese designer
in Paris in 2015.

"N endo" means "modeling clay" in Japanese. The term gave its name to the working group founded in 2002 by Oki Sato, shortly after graduating in architecture from Waseda University in Tokyo, together with fifteen colleagues who met during their university studies. Active in the field of interior design, furnishing and graphics, Nendo is characterized by a supple and flexible approach to design, combining creative potential with the childlike surprise of simplicity.

Discovered by Giulio Cappellini at Milan's Salone Satellite in 2004, the Japanese design firm has done a number of products for the Italian company, in a ten-year partnership celebrated in 2015 with an exhibition that recounted its course from the beginning. Their works are invariably characterized by light forms and the irony of gravity-defying furniture.

Their first joint product, after a year spent experimenting and prototyping, was the *Yuki* screen, presented at the 2006 Salone del Mobile in Milan. This consisted of plastic modules in the form of snowflakes (*yuki* in Japanese) which can be assembled in compositions of different sizes.

Nendo always combines an ironic and playful idea, effectively expressed in its drawings, with careful research into materials, seeking to economize in their use and tracing them as light, evanescent lines. So the *Ribbon* stools (2007) are made of laser-cut sheet metal, folded and lacquered glossy white, black, red, yellow or blue. Evidence of their stability is inspired by the interlacing of the ribbons of ballet shoes. The *Thin Black Table* (2011) is a low geometric form made out of two intersecting offset cubes balanced on the slenderest of profiles, with a system of joints and transparencies reminiscent of an Escher drawing. The *Bambi* table (2008) defies gravity, its name evoking the precarious stability of the legs of a fawn. The basic idea was to create a desk from a single plane, folded in different directions. Its stability is ensured by the opposed angles of the two legs, intersecting at 90 degrees.

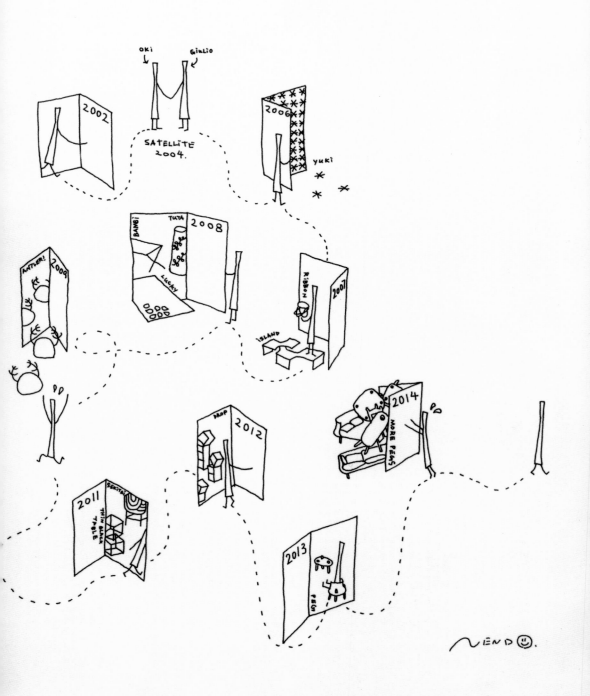

The *Island* table (2007) works on the lightness of the material inspired by the moment when the water level rises with the tides, so that what looked like a solid mass of earth turns into a seascape dotted with islands. The table consists of two elements of different heights and sizes, laser cut out of sheet metal, folded and painted white or black. Assembled they make up a variety of "archipelagos."

The *Drop* double-sided bookcase (2012) plays on an inclination of 45 degrees of the topmost shelf, which seems to be precariously balanced on one side and at the same time offers a variety of possibilities for storing books. A feature of this project was the studies of a Nendo color palette. "Working with the designers also means provoking them," observes Giulio. "While other designers work a lot with color, Nendo like black and white. Then I asked them to introduce other colors. They came back to me with a palette of many colors and said: 'Now choose.' We chose three shades—pink, blue and beige—inspired by the colors of nature in Japan, such as the pink of the cherry blossoms, and the gray river-smoothed stones. Working with Nendo takes me back to my encounter with Shiro **Kuramata** and his great rigor, poetic lightness and clean lines. We have developed a series of successful projects, poised between real and unreal."

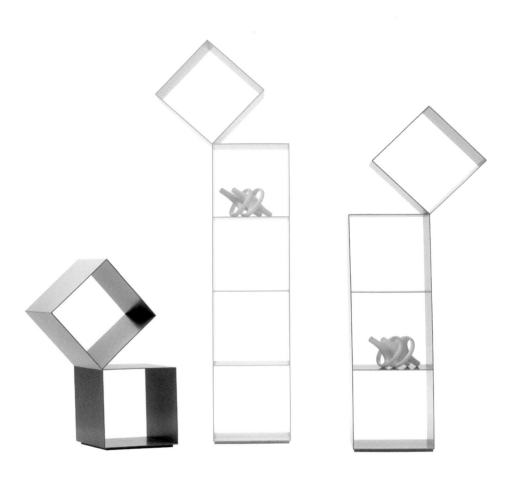

Nendo, *Drop* (2012).
Studies and three variants
of the bookcase.

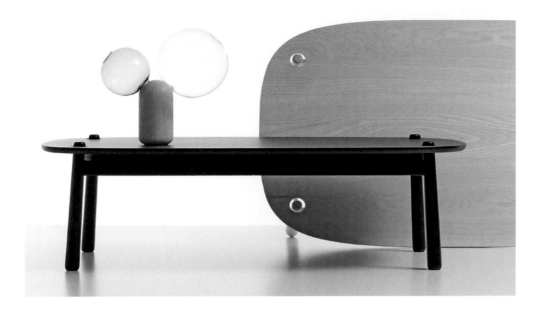

Above: Nendo, *Peg* coffee table (2014–2015).

Opposite: Picture of Oki Sato, founder
of the Nendo office with Akihiro Ito.

NEWSON

Marc Newson,
Wooden Chair (1988).

G iulio Cappellini is meticulous about detail. This shows in the way Marc Newson began working with his company. In one of those odd moments spent browsing magazines, where he sometimes spots interesting new designers, Cappellini happened to pick up an Australian magazine and saw a small picture of a cafeteria: the Pod Bar in Roppongi, Tokyo. This was Newson's first interior design during his years in the Japanese capital, soon after founding his design studio, POD, which gave its name not only to the café but also to his first products. What tweaked the Italian entrepreneur's interest was the detail of the handle Newson had designed for the door into this bar, a simple glass door with a steel frame but astonishingly refined. Cappellini sent him a plane ticket to Italy, the start of a period when they worked closely and became friends. "He said he never wanted to become an industrial designer but an artist. Perhaps because of this, his sculptural propensity and care for materials, the autonomy of forms with small production runs gave rise to products that were interesting stylistically and technically." The relation between Newson and Cappellini became a true partnership, with their shared willingness to take risks, experiment and create new languages receptive to the **dream** with a hint of irony.

Fascinated by natural forms and technological materials, and more deeply immersed in the art world than industrial design, Newson designs sculptural objects, initially one-off pieces or limited series produced by Idée. The Australian designer's first concern is not with people but the shape of an object, the true focus of the environment, which people somehow have "to adapt to". His works have become icons of contemporary life for their ability to shape volumes and model material, for their hollow and rounded forms kindled by brilliant colors, a Pop taste and a design language that is created by inventing and using a new design vocabulary.

After the success of *Lockheed Lounge* and *Pod of Drawers*, both made of aluminum, *Embryo* was one of the first projects to experiment with mono-material, sinuous forms made from a different type of material. Polyurethane foam coated with neoprene shapes the shell of the seat and back, from which project three steel "legs," actually the extremities of a single frame that creates a single whole with the seat itself, like limbs inseparable from the body. Designed for the exhibition *Take a Seat* at the Powerhouse Museum in Sydney (1988), the chair was originally made in a limited series by Idée— the design workshop conceived and directed by Teruo Kurosaki which Newson started working with in his years spent in Japan— and was the first to be produced in Europe by Cappellini.

The *Wooden Chair* embodies the maximum of curvature that can be achieved with specific woods and also the level of experimentation and hazard typical of both designer and producer. Conceived for an exhibition in Sydney of chairs made out of wood, a material abundant in Australia, it had required difficult research to make the transition from design to creation of the prototype. After searching in vain for a local craftsman willing to make the chair, Newson managed to find a carpenter in Tasmania who was willing to do it, using curved pine strips. Based on the flexibility of the material, both in terms of construction and use, inflecting under the human weight, it consists of paired strips of wood, each different in length and curvature, for which special templates are needed. The profiles are then assembled manually and screwed into place,

Opposite: Marc Newson, *Embryo Chair* (1988).

Above: Marc Newson, *Orgone* (1991).

with a process that involves technical expertise and craftsmanship.

Newson's projects are governed by geometry and movement, conceived in three dimensions in keeping with principles of morphological homogeneity and manipulation of **matter**. If the idea is given a shape through digital modeling and stereolithography, the engineering is the result of a continuous exchange of ideas between the designer and the company. Compositional control, materials and finishes are subjected to continuous reinventions generated by the interaction between different skills that lead to the final design.

A chaise longue in fiberglass molded in a single piece with three conical feet, *Orgone*—with its linear profile and bright colors, like a board for riding the waves—is a tribute to Newson's passion for surfing. But it is also an evolution of *Embryo*, whose forms are

"flattened" as if crushed by a steamroller. It would become a new design icon, a prototype of experiments and unusual products which had already determined the choice of name. "Orgone," in English "orgon," is a term coined by the Austrian psychoanalyst Wilhelm Reich to name the alleged elementary particle of cosmic life energy. From here on it would also identify the hourglass form recurrent in the Australian designer's projects, used both as a generator of objects and a pattern.

Often described as organic and inclined to biomorphism, Newson's work is actually difficult to pigeonhole because of the continuous search for a personal language that relates the natural and scientific world to the study of technology, symmetry and matter, experimenting on scales ranging from airplanes to interior design and all the way down to the tumbler.

NORGUET

Patrick Norguet,
Rive Droite (2001).

The career of Patrick Norguet owes much to Giulio Cappellini, who brought him into the limelight in 1999 by producing his *Rainbow Chair*. Norguet's work hybridizes fashion and design in way that the Italian company has always theorized, creating products that enhance and showcase both.

The meeting between the two was due to Cristina Morozzi. One evening she showed Giulio an example of the chair made of colorful slats that the designer had presented at the Paris furniture fair. "I asked her for his phone number and tried to contact him. When we finally got him on the line it was midnight. I told him I'd seen his prototype and wanted to produce it. He kept slamming the phone down, thinking it was a friend playing a practical joke on him. The next morning we met and that gave rise to our first product."

Characterized by the contrast between simple lines and brilliant coloring, the *Rainbow Chair* is turned out by an innovative process that, once again, brings together sophisticated technological processes and craftsmanship. The chair is made entirely of methacrylate, comprising slats of eleven different colors and seven different thicknesses assembled with an ultrasound system

so as to avoiding drops of glue being seen in it.

The slats are cut out with a panel saw for greater accuracy. CNC machines are used to precision slice the forty-four sections to be assembled. After this fabrication, the chair is fully hand crafted. The sections from the second stage of processing are first stacked and glued to form the seat and back, then joined to the profile of the legs. The chair is now completely glued, but still not smooth and shiny, with the colors still concealed by the still opaque surface. Abrasive cloths are used to give the product a surface smooth to the touch. Then long and careful buffing brings out the characteristic colors of the *Rainbow Chair*, making them glow in all their beauty and transparency.

After the success of this chair, Cappellini and Norguet worked together to design an upholstered armchair which would perfectly fuse design and fashion in a rather simple and compact form with graphic and colorful patterns. "Looking at the archive of Emilio Pucci's designer materials, we found, in his notebooks, some original patterns developed for fabrics, which we used to cover Nourget's chair." In shades of blue, yellow and violet, the *Rive Droite* armchair, launched in 2001, has a vintage feel, evoking the fashions of the glorious sixties and celebrating a blend of fashion and design.

Patrick Norguet,
Rainbow Chair (1999).
As some other objects
by Cappellini, this chair is part
of the permanent collection
at MoMA, New York.

OGGETTO (PROGETTO OGGETTO)

OBJECT (PROGETTO OGGETTO)

Progetto Oggetto, presentation of the first collection at Carugo, 1992. The products are displayed in a "virtual" setting with white lines evoking the presence of furniture and architectural elements.

In the late eighties, there was a gap in the design market corresponding to the home accessory. In the past this was a tradition that had produced some significant achievements, but it was then lost and supplanted by larger items and furnishings.

The idea of creating "a collection of small objects, some necessary, others not, for everyday use in the home," was devised almost as a pastime during the long conversations between the designers in those years. Cappellini's interlocutors in this case were Jasper **Morrison** and James Irvine. The former had only just started his busy partnership with Cappellini and whenever he visited Milan he would stay with his friend Irvine, who had moved there after graduating, like him, from the Royal College of Art. So it was that Giulio also met James.

One morning he went to pick up Jasper and take him to his office in Brianza and a stranger in boxers and T-shirt opened the door to him.

So began a very intense personal and professional relationship between the three of them. Together they began to reflect on this collective project. "At first the idea grew up as a joke, and we spent our free time on it. I remember our first get-togethers on Lake Como. We would pick up James and Jasper at Carugo station, have lunch in a restaurant and continue, with long talks, on a bench in the square, where we put together our ideas of what would become **Progetto Oggetto** and the **people** we thought we could get involved in it."

Progetto Oggetto was an opportunity to launch a line of practical products, small in size but also to put together a schedule of different ways of thinking about design on a small scale.

Jasper Morrison, *3 Green Bottles* (1992) for *Progetto Oggetto*.

Opposite: 1992 presentation of some objects from the first collection *Progetto Oggetto*.

It was a collective experiment in interdisciplinary design, coordinated by Jasper in London and James in Milan. Behind it all lay the idea of involving different people from around the world, with a deliberately international approach: each of the designers involved had total freedom in terms of product, materials and technology, and especially in terms of expression. Respect for different viewpoints was crucial, as was the desire not to establish a single style, but to express the complexity of the languages of that circuit of young designers who were renewing the field. The objects were then made by Brianza-based craftsmen, working in very different areas of **production**. "We got the glass vases by Marc **Newson** blown on Murano, we involved the extraordinary ceramist Alessio Sarri,

we traveled in the area around Brescia to identify experts at working sheet metal."

The spirit of sharing extended to every aspect of the project: from the choice of designer products to catalogues and **exhibitions**. This gave rise to a variety of languages and design attitudes, in a climate of debate and reflection that was the heart of the process.

The first presentation of *Progetto Oggetto* was at the company's headquarters at Carugo, in Brianza, in 1992. Real objects created a dialogue with a virtual environment, in which the architectural elements and furnishings were designed with a white line on the walls, reversing the change of scale: starting from the small home accessory they tried to imagine the setting of life in the **home**.

PERSONE

PEOPLE

S ynergies with people are the essence of a project capable of communicating and asserting its strength. Especially among those engaged in different sectors, discussion triggers the synergies needed if the company is to grow.

The company's history is marked by numerous encounters. Whether with youngsters at their first experience of design or established figures from around the world, day by day Cappellini has built up a network of enthusiastic talents of different ages and backgrounds. The important thing is that they all have feelings they want to convey so as to reach a common goal: designs that express emotions. But Cappellini's achievement also includes many people from outside the design world, who have enriched its kaleidoscopic project ever since its inception.

"Getting to know new people in Europe and around the world, with widely different backgrounds and identities, has always been a great stimulus, something that has taught me a lot, given me a lot. Meetings with notables, like Queen Elizabeth, and those with characters like Romeo Gigli, Mika or Paul Smith, have always been valuable opportunities for dialogue and discussion. All these individuals, from the most ordinary to the most important, are an important source of growth personally and professionally."

Giulio Cappellini has no doubt that looking through the eyes of people outside the industry and measuring yourself with them opens the mind. "An outside look reveals limitations and unexplored potential. It helps you reflect and focus on the only task we have: to make products for the public, recount dreams and set them smiling."

Giulio Cappellini and Queen
Elizabeth on her visit to Italy
in 2000.

POST-INDUSTRIALE

POST-INDUSTRIAL

Raw Edges, *TWB – Tailored Wood Bench* (2010). The particular method of fabrication and filling of the product makes each piece different from the others.

E very object in the Cappellini catalogue tells a story that is not just of a form but also of a process, often blending craftsmanship and technology. In the encounter between these two practices, the art director today sees the excellence of the design and the interpretation of contemporary taste. A sophisticated and technologically advanced production system allows each piece to look like a one-off product, made by hand. This is what can be called a post-industrial system.

It is the natural evolution of the traditional craftsmanship that consolidated the myth of Italian products in the fifties. Making products today with the same quality as then means recognizing the central role of craftsmanship while reinventing its relationship with high-tech industrial processes.

Some designers have turned their research in this direction, and their projects have not escaped Giulio Cappellini's watchful eye. The work of Nipa Doshi and Jonathan Levien, who designed the *Capo* chair for Cappellini, perfectly embodies the encounter between craft tradition and technological **innovation**. He is British, with a concern for comfort and the needs of production, an approach typical of industrial design. She is Indian, refined in the use of materials, and continuously

searching for the tailored details which will distinguish their products. Together they possess a sensibility and skills that are perfectly complementary, combining a love for what is unique and hand-crafted with the precision and hardness of an industrial product.

From this point of view the *Tailored Wood Bench* stool designed by Raw Edges is likewise a perfect interpretation of the post-industrial society. The work of the Israeli designers is based on the encounter between industrial hand-crafted objects and the attempt to modernize traditional techniques so as to use them in innovative ways. The stool consists of a veneer filled with expanded polyurethane foam: in expanding, the foam deforms the wood veneer and gives it a form that looks as if it had been sculpted and shaped by hand. The principle is similar to that used to make the *Mr. B* series of seats by **Azambourg:** a slender laminate (of wood for Raw Edges, of metal for Azambourg) is folded and injected with foam. Depending on how the object is moved, the foam acts differently and so the shape also changes.

This kind of process, in which highly industrialized methods require the intervention of skilled craftsmanship, it is also common to iconic products in the Cappellini catalogue, like Patrick **Norguet**'s *Rainbow Chair*, Marcel **Wanders**' *Knotted Chair* or Jasper **Morrison**'s *Hi Pad* chairs.

Please Tell Us How to Make a Rainbow Chair

Stages of production of Patrick Norguet's *Rainbow Chair*. The first two phases use machinery to slice the sections (using a panel saw) and the separate pieces to be glued (with CNC machinery). After this it is completed by hand with the assembly and the buffing of the material to bring out the glowing colors.

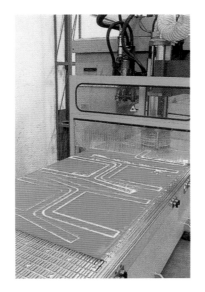

PRODUZIONE

PRODUCTION

You cannot design if you don't know the production structure and how it functions **concretely**. For those who work in the company's R&D office, every project is a new invention and a challenge. It involves identifying a strategy to make it excellent in production terms, without altering the original design, in a long process of mediation between the company's needs, the designer, the manufacturer and the market. The activities that precede production include analysis of the competition, development of the concept and formal research, material analysis, a feasibility study, drafting the technical drawings for the design, preliminary prototyping and the definitive solution; engineering, structural tests, tests of materials, and finally the creation of a pre-series.

Cappellini products are the result of very different production processes. Some are adapted to high technological standards and manufactured in series out of plastic or metal, using molds and various kinds of sophisticated equipment. Others are made in limited quantities almost entirely by hand. Still others are a mix of technology and craftsmanship, following the traces of Italian know-how with an entirely contemporary outlook that is essentially **post-industrial**.

Production of the *Lotus* chair by Jasper Morrison.

In this process, the relationship with the suppliers is important. It favors those who do not work for other companies so that they develop (and retain) an attitude and precision in the way they work that is only found at Cappellini. Most of them are located in Brianza, near the company headquarters, with the exception of certain specific technologies or projects engaged with multiculturalism and the promotion of distant craft practices, such as "Mondo" or "Cappellini Love". Some of these workshops offer real surprises. One of the most interesting stories, in this respect, is that of Tom Dixon's *S Chair*. This icon, which has now entered the history of design, is produced in a small workshop in Brianza, set in a farmhouse, with a barnyard full of animals outside. Here the straw coating is applied to the metal structure. The same chair, by contrast, is then also turned out using

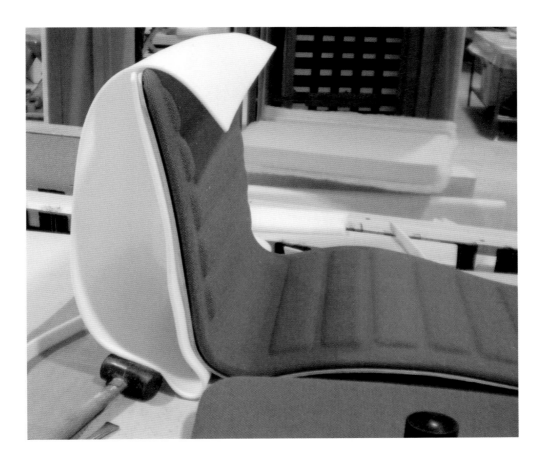

much more sophisticated production techniques in fabric or leather versions.

"In working with many designers, you have to learn the thoughts and concerns of each, to understand which features you have to insist on in adapting their initial design. Some are extremely meticulous and even a degree or a millimeter of difference in the final result is unacceptable," says Stefano Barbazza, head of R&D. "To Giulio it's essential to understand the way they think and how they see their projects. It's only then that he directs them, according to his needs and those of the company."

It may not be obvious at first glance, but if you look at each product in the Cappellini catalogue carefully, you find that it is a challenge to the limits of **matter** and engineering. Examples range from the development of decorative or functional details to more structural solutions. Hence

the *Ribbon* stools designed by **Nendo** have a clear plastic coating that looks like glass to support the feet, and a hidden magnet that ensures the little cushion on the seat stays in place. The *Bambi* table does not have a low upright. It stands up because the side legs are rotated in relation to each other and the central core bulges. The *Deco Doors* system, designed by Marcel **Wanders** for Cappellini *Systems* in 2013, led to the development of a revolutionary technique to create the three-dimensional pattern. With the touch of a hot mold, the decoration is imprinted on the panel creating an embossed pattern in relief and a very evocative chiaroscuro effect, unique on the market. These are just some of the results of Cappellini's technological research, with its gift for **innovation** and experimenting with new solutions. Each object conceals its secret, its history and a challenge.

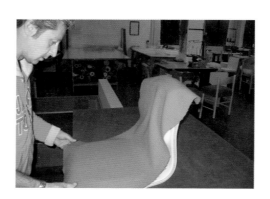

Some stages in the production of Jasper Morrison's *Hi Pad* chairs:
application of the fabric or leather upholstery, hand-pressed to ensure
it follows the shape of the foam padding. The surplus fabric is inserted
into the special slit on the peripheral edge of the wooden frame,
matching the front part with that on the back. Then the edge is closed
with a profile made of the same type of fabric or leather.

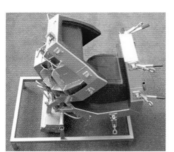
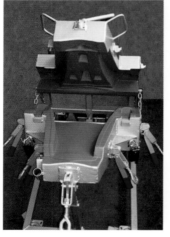

Molds used to make the *Spring* chair, designed in 2000
by Erwan Bouroullec. The base is made of brushed stainless steel
and the shell of rigid molded polyurethane with polyurethane
foam padding, with upholstery in the fabrics and leathers
of the collection.

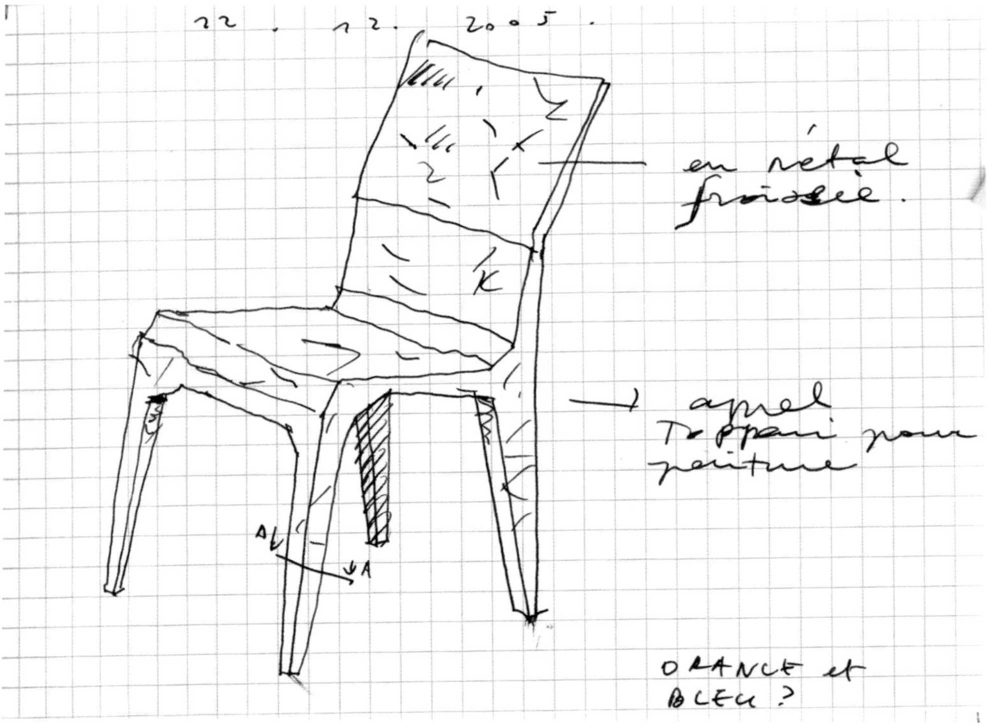

22 . 22 . 2005 .

en métal
froissée.

apel
Toppaui pour
peinture

ORANCE et
BLEU ?

François Azambourg, a study of the *Mr. B* chair and phases
of production: the sheet metal shapes, previously cut and beaten
by hand, are bent, welded and then injected with polyurethane foam.

RISCHIO

RISK

"Only enthusiasm enables you to win challenges. The challenges for us, here at Cappellini, consist of working with a new constructive team outlook, while maintaining our position on a difficult market, penalized by the recession, and continuing to be proactive and innovative. **Innovation** is the element to which we devote our greatest energy and it gives us our greatest sense of fulfillment. The success of *Superoblong*, the new unstructured sofa devised by Jasper **Morrison**, is a practical example. Challenges are won with action and not talk." So Giulio Cappellini in 2004, relaunched the business after a management change that made it part of the Poltrona Frau Group, the pilot of a project in the "new pole of beauty" supported by Charme, Luca Cordero di Montezemolo's investment company.

He always remembers that it's impossible to believe profoundly in what you're doing unless you're willing to take risks. "Risk is an integral part of work based on innovation and choices made with the heart more than the head."

In Cappellini's history risk is ever-present. The curiosity of its art director is embodied in the courage to take risks: to invest in unknown names, to give scope and confidence to young people, to open up new markets, launch new trends, create new combinations. Or again, risk is bound up with Giulio's moods. As he himself acknowledges, he might fall in love with something and then hate it a week later. But risk is also a consequence of irony, leading you to present objects that can be loved as well as openly criticized, investing in a mind like that of Fabio Novembre, and in products that are so powerful that other companies would never consider them.

Risk involves questions of taste, research into engineering, the selection of products and materials. Once the company produced up to one hundred products a year, and they would be displayed at **exhibitions** in huge, bloated venues. Today it creates a smaller number of products and the ordering system has changed. It no longer takes part in large events but creates more settings closer to its clients, easily replicable in their distribution in different parts of the world. The challenge today is to send a strong message, instantly comprehensible yet surprising.

Milano Design Village 2010,
at the Fuorisalone in Milan.

SHOWROOM

Cappellini showrooms around the world. At right New York (USA) and Ho Chi Minh City (Vietnam).

T he identity of a company that started from Brianza and has become an international leader, making its way across all kinds of boundaries, finds its strength in the knowledge that it is recognizable because it knows how to be eclectic and many-sided. This principle also guided its progressive opening of new showrooms, in Milan, Paris, Los Angeles, New York, Sidney and Manila, reflecting the brand's expansion around the world. "Our job is to sell the same products everywhere, though perhaps with different finishes, textures, colors and details. The perception of color in London is very different from that of the same color in Miami. In the showroom we try to represent our products with images that are not always uniform, and especially to embed them in the local culture. **People** live in all sorts of different ways. Trying to relate the products to their way of life and thinking is fundamental," observes Cappellini, strong in the belief that we should look to the future without ever effacing tradition. "Imposing a product designed and manufactured in Italy on a country with a completely different culture and history would be an act of violence. We make products for people, and we have to take their cultural heritage into account."

The choice of products to be exhibited or sold and the finishes adopted in different parts of the world is increasingly weighted towards the identities of the places, people and cultures that inhabit them, their history, tastes and markets. The challenge is to make the presence of Cappellini recognizable anywhere in the world without giving up the differences and without damping its creativity, reinventing itself through the stimuli and sensations absorbed from the local culture.

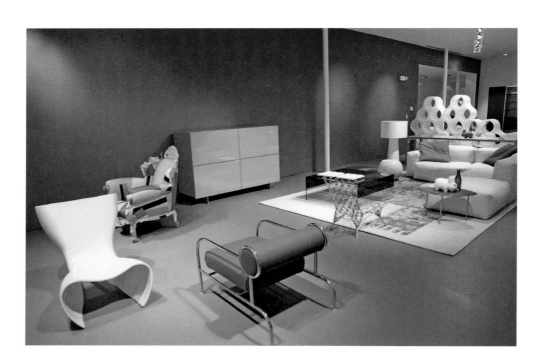

Miami (USA), Abu Dhabi
(UAE).

Milan (Italy), Paris (France).

SOGNO

DREAM

Exhibition *Cappellini's Dream*, 2006.

Weaving between rationality and fantasy, design has to be able to set **people** dreaming. This belief guides and directs Giulio Cappellini's work and the decisions of the company, which seeks to create products that liberate the imagination and cause a stir. The relationship between the individual and design should not be aesthetic, in Cappellini's philosophy, but rather overwhelming and emotional. Each object has to be able to generate a memory, a thought, an emotion, until it becomes a part of everyday life.

The company's project is the embodiment of a dream: to host in the **home** the creations of the great names of international industrial design, following the guide of an innate curiosity, passion and openness to all forms of expression.

This is the dream that Cappellini recounts at every event and presentation: seeking to display his objects not aseptically but so as to touch emotional chords. This is why his exhibit designs create an atmosphere and are never commercial displays. Just think of the smoke enveloping the objects by Shiro **Kuramata** at the Museo di Milano in 1986, the candles that guided visitors through the streets of Carugo to the company's doors, the contrast between the installations and the brownfield sites chosen for many **exhibitions**, the custodians of stories and lives now completed but brought back to life by the presence of design." One of the comments that made me happiest in the history of our productions," recalls Giulio, "was made by an elderly couple at the Fabbrica del Vapore, at a show we did

there in 1992. One day they met me and said: 'This is the third time we've come to see the exhibition. We're not really into design but whenever we come here, for half an hour we can dream'."

So in 2006 the theme of the exhibition presented in the **showroom** on Via Santa Cecilia in Milan during the Salone del Mobile was just that: *Cappellini's Dream*. A journey through design recounted through the projects that have helped fulfill that dream. The *Thinking Man's Chair* represented all the calm and reflectiveness of a great project by Jasper **Morrison**; the *Proust* armchair transmitted the visionary power of Alessandro Mendini; The *Wooden Chair* by Marc **Newson**, which faced Cappellini with a new technological and material challenge, or the classic revisited with great irony by Marcel **Wanders** in the *New Antiques* line of chairs, tables and coffee tables. A dream of a show, which toured various exhibition venues, taking with it the most significant pieces in the collection. And, like some nineteenth-century traveler's luggage, they moved from place to place enclosed in large wooden crates, the custodians of memories, enriched from time to time with the new places they went to.

"Cappellini invites us to dream. His design pieces, capable of bringing together images of the past, moments of the present and thoughts of the future, are our guides." A dream which comes to life in the encounters with other people, his faith in the products, the **innovation** carried on through the work of every day. A "reasoned dream" that is the secret hidden within the company's history.

Thinking Man's Chair
Jasper Morrison

La calma di un grand progetto

Exhibition *Cappellini's Dream*,
2006.

SUPERSTUDIO

Superstudio, 2000.

T he 1992 installation at the Fabbrica del Vapore marked a new direction for design presentations by occupying an abandoned factory and asserting the prominence of events off the trade fair site. With an even greater impact in some ways, since 2000 the Superstudio venue in Via Tortona has become an important hub of Milan's Design Week, after Cappellini was the first to use it as an exhibition center. This area of Milan, occupied by industries that were still active in the eighties, was characterized architecturally and socially by its factories and workshops. After the factories closed and moved away, the abandoned sheds were gradually taken over by artists, designers and photographers, who converted them into workshops and studios, real clusters of fashion, design and art with an international appeal. Giulio Cappellini recalls when Gisella Borioli and her husband Flavio Lucchini bought this old brownfield site, starting with Superstudio 13 and then enlarging it to take in Superstudio Più. And he remembers the day when, a few weeks before the Milan furniture fair—at a time when company had already fixed its schedule of events—Gisella Borioli called him and asked if he could do something to promote this space. "This derelict factory left me feeling astonished and stimulated. I told her I didn't just want to do something, I intended to move the firm's whole presentation there for the duration of the Salone del Mobile." For some years, from 2000 to 2004, there followed a series of memorable productions in this spacious venue, used to recount the story of the new collections and young talents selected by Cappellini.

In 2000 it presented a display with installations dedicated to each designer. All the novelties that year—about forty in all—were presented on mirror-finish daises, with different installations depending on the kind of product. There were chairs stacked high, pieces of furniture set side by side or containers positioned vertically, and between one platform and the other, the aisles running through the otherwise huge space were marked by filters made from colored tissue paper. In the following years the company has always reinterpreted itself by following the concept of a series of installations, objects and different designers. In 2004 the display took the form of one of those homes that crop up regularly in Cappellini's displays: a **home** where the products of the new and the old collection were combined to show what could be done with the company's catalogue, and how the Cappellini range could be used to furnish a whole house.

Above: Superstudio, 2000.

Opposite: Superstudio, 2001.

Memorable parties would be thrown on the evenings before the inauguration of the Salone, organized as blazing openings to the Design Week, with thousands and thousands of **people** taking part.

"Today it no longer makes sense to hold big events. We need more closely focused initiatives that target the final public, trying to give them what they expect," acknowledges Giulio. "But those events certainly made a break with the presentations of good Milanese design. They offered a lively alternative to the secluded events held in **showrooms** in the center of town, which did nothing to open up the event

to the city and the general public. The Cappellini parties at Superstudio were meant to favor participation and communication."

Superstudio continued to change and improve. The space was transformed and became well known. It began to lose the appearance of a derelict factory, and the installations changed as a result, becoming more highly finished in various ways. But Cappellini is convinced the most memorable presentations were those made when it was still a big abandoned factory, and the designer objects, colors and forms created settings with a tremendous visual impact.

TALENT
SCOUTING

S—
ince the beginning
of the eighties, when Giulio
Cappellini began to travel and
entertain wider ambitions for
the family business (declared
in the very name, expanded
into Cappellini International Interiors),
the company has become a design landmark
worldwide. Discovering still unknown talents and
making them names recognized internationally
has become one of his main activities,
transforming the brand into the "**dream**" of many
young people just out of school. By broadening
the vision of companies that, a few decades
earlier, had affirmed the value of home-grown
designers of the generation of Gae Aulenti,
Achille **Castiglioni** and Vico Magistretti,
bringing together creative potential and industrial
capacity, Giulio Cappellini threw open the doors
of the consolidated empyrean of Italian design
to Europe and the world. By investing in young
Brits, Australians, Japanese and French with
entrepreneurial courage and an extraordinary
instinct, he launched the first collaborations with
designers such as Jasper **Morrison** and Tom

Dixon. These partnerships were based on a shared
passion and the desire for **innovation**, flowing
not only into the **production** of objects but
enduring success stories.

Believing in new talents and wagering on
them has become an integral part of the history
of Cappellini, which invests time, money and
energy in the search for names that can make
a contribution to the development of design.

Sketches, drawings, letters and proposals have
always flowed in to the company offices, where
they are collected and stored in whole cabinets.
Formerly Giulio used to examine the projects one
by one and meet in person the young people who
came to see him to exchange ideas. Today close
attention is still paid to the proposals, which are
sifted and passed to the art director, and then any
appointments will be fixed during the Salone del
Mobile in Milan.

But the most important selection, the one
most likely to lead to new collaborations,
is driven by curiosity and the watchful eye
of Cappellini himself, arising out of his travels
and chance meetings. At trade **fairs**, lectures,
exhibitions, or the pages of magazines, an object

Following pages: Giulio
Cappellini and the young
designers selected for
"Cappellini Next" at the Design
Village installed in the spaces
of the former Fondazione
Pomodoro by Poltrona Frau
Group for the Salone del
Mobile 2012.

will catch his eye and suggest that whoever
designed it has potential.

"It doesn't matter whether a designer
is 20 years old or 60, whether they were born
in Milan or Mumbai. The important thing
is how good they are," as Giulio Cappellini
always says. "There's no precise way to find
new talent. I'm curious, I travel a lot and
I'm interested in meeting **people**. I'm often
invited as a visiting professor to universities
and design schools. I'm the creative director
of the Istituto Marangoni design school and
I sit on competition juries, so I always have
opportunities to view projects by students and
youthful designers. Often just a detail will catch
my attention. The key issue is then to be able
to establish a good rapport with the different
designers, respecting their histories, cultures and
traditions, and letting yourself be influenced
by their characters."

Few projects directly presented by a designer
then go into a production. One of the most
recent exceptions is Bakery Studio, who were
at the trade fair during the Salone del Mobile
in Milan in 2010, exhibiting their work at

the Salone Satellite (the independent designers'
showcase). They left a catalogue at the Cappellini
showroom with their photo on the cover.
The next day Giulio Cappellini recognized
them at a chance encounter, followed
by the collaboration that the following year
led to the production of *NOM*, an exaltation
of design work that starts from a study of **matter**.

A concern with the young and the enrichment
that comes from exchanging ideas with
them emerges from Giulio's constant openness
to all those who, after a lecture or press
conference, come up and show him a project,
perhaps just a prototype photographed with
a smartphone. Giulio Cappellini always does
his best to listen and give advice and would
probably like to find space for many more young
people than is possible. For many designers,
Cappellini still means opportunity, a safe
launch pad that will pave the way to success
or perhaps a crucial encounter. With the hope
that one day, maybe, they might just receive
a visit or a phone call from Giulio himself.
After all, that was how Morrison, **Wanders**
and many others got started.

TEAM

The individual paths followed by the designers and the products turned out by the company are backed by an ensemble, which rests on the exchanges between different personalities. Founded as a family business, over the years, Cappellini grew until it had nearly 200 employees in the early 2000s and then returned to being a team of a few dozen **people**. At least two of its staff joined the company in the same years as the current art director, reminders of the inclusive family character of its early days and the way the structure has changed, introducing new hierarchies and new dynamics. They recall the importance of the role of Mrs Cappellini, Giulio's mother, with her strong and determined character, who was responsible for sales. They recall his father and brother, who ran the technical and production sides, and of course young Giulio, primarily engaged in marketing.

Though the company has grown, teamwork remains crucial. In the early years, when it had the dimensions of a small craft business, everyone turned their hand to practically everything. Then, over time, the way the business was run also changed. "Working at Cappellini, especially in the past, meant multitasking whatever your job. Not only filling orders or doing secretarial work when necessary, but also learning to get by on your own in various ways, with a heavy burden of responsibility and plenty of opportunities to grow professionally," recount the firm's early employees. They convey their sense of the great good luck of working in a business which gave them a comprehensive view of everything that was happening and way production meshed with work in the offices.

Giulio Cappellini is described by all his colleagues as a highly charismatic, inspirational figure. He will often throw a project into chaos by suddenly changing direction and driving his staff to achieve more, but infusing them with renewed energy and enthusiasm by passing from outbursts to moments of extreme charm. The decisive figure in every decision that is taken, he participates as much as possible in the daily work, in a relationship of exchanges that were once the focus of the work and still remain strong even in recent years, now the brand has become part of a group.

But Giulio's centralizing presence is actually the pivot of a system based on freedom and the delegation of responsibilities, that allows everyone to believe in what they are doing and give their utmost, looking for the best way to achieve their targets. Freedom feeds passion, enthusiasm and sharing. And with its dimensions of a large family business, the collaborative spirit that finds its strength in the contact and the group has held the company together even in the most difficult times and still animates it today.

For his part, Giulio believes strongly in the need for teamwork and to share decision-making, problems and achievements. "I know I'm not easy to work with. I always try to get the most out of others and I involve those who are in the company in the effort to do their best. People expect a lot of us and it's our duty to give it. In the end, if things go well it's because we've all done a good job, and if there are problems we all have to put ourselves on the line." Sharing processes and decisions is as much about marketing, involved in communication and the expression of the brand, as product development. And it is important not to overlook the team outside the company, the outer circle of skilled craft businesses whose expertise solves problems of **production**, with their staff often working through Saturdays and Sundays and putting in all-nighters in the effort to attain things that seemed impossible.

"I don't like an isolating attitude and I think that the truly successful project is the result of teamwork between different people. I like to give scope to young minds and, although often I start by telling them bluntly they're wrong, because I feel my convictions are shaken, I always try to learn from what I'm told. I look and try to understand how their ideas can enter the greater Cappellini project. Relations with the people involved in research and development are vital. I like to oversee the way products grow out of the original idea to the final outcome. As a good architect and a creative, I love to express opinions, pitch ideas and throw my weight about. Those who've been working with me for many years now know exactly what suits me and my pet aversions. Often, surprisingly enough, they turn out products exactly as I would have wanted them. The industry cannot live without craft skills. I'm grateful to all the craft workers, inside and outside the firm, who give the best of their energies and feel proud to be part of a great shared project."

Giulio Cappellini with his team
in the workshops at Lentate
(premises of the R&D
department) and the offices
at Meda.

WANDERS

Marcel Wanders, *Knotted Chair*
(1996).

"A t the start of a collaboration
I always enjoy calling on
designers to see where
and how they work and
look around their studios.
Sometimes they're big
workshops, others are simple caverns. In 1996,
when I saw the prototype of the *Knotted
Chair* published in a magazine, I at once tried
to contact the designer." So Giulio Cappellini
went to Amsterdam to meet Marcel Wanders,
who for the occasion had borrowed a room from
a friend to show off his prototypes to the best
advantage. Cappellini indicated the ones he
was interested in and a few weeks later, during
the lunch break, a young Dutchman turned up
at the firm's shipping department and asked
to see him. "It was Marcel Wanders who had
rented a van, loaded all the prototypes he had
developed into it and brought them to show
me first hand. He told me to wait ten minutes
until he organized them in a nice display
so I could view them. That's how we started
working together." Passion, commitment and
perseverance soon made him into a great
international star.

Initially designed for Droog Design,
the *Knotted Chair* went well in **production**
thanks to Giulio Cappellini's sharp eye.
It has become a contemporary classic, now
in the permanent collections of museums
around the world. The starting point is a design,
a simple insight that has shaped one of the best-
known design icons of recent times: a synthetic
cord made of aramid with a carbon fiber core
is knotted into the shape of a chair. The slack
web is impregnated with epoxy resin and
hung from a frame to harden, leaving gravity
the task of giving the product its final and
permanent form. It is a chair that never ceases
to intrigue the viewer, even twenty years after
it was invented. By combining industrial and
craft techniques, it unites the fascination
of lightness with perfect solidity.

After devising the *Knotted Chair*, Marcel
Wanders has designed many other objects for
Cappellini. Working on the synthesis between
technology and craftsmanship, between
simplicity and sophistication, Wanders creates
light, ironic products starting from a knowledge
of materials and their potential to experiment
with new processes.

Marcel Wanders, *Tulip Armchair* (2010). Exhibition at Mira Moon Hotel, Hong Kong.

Following pages: left, Marcel Wanders, *New Antiques* chairs (2005) in the black version. Right, Marcel Wanders, *Big Shadow* (1998, *Progetto Oggetto*).

One example is *Big Shadow*, a floor lamp made of white PVC in 1998 and revived over the years in different colors and limited editions, replacing the sobriety of monochromatic fabrics with the exuberance of colors and textures. In *Eye Shadow* (2013), what at first glance looks like a drawing of an Art Deco stained-glass window, on closer inspection turns out to be a multitude of eyes and pupils in macro format printed with brilliant colors.

Equally fascinating are two seats in the shape of flowers: *Tulip Armchair* (2010) and *Dalia* (2013) are two giant calyxes that evoke corollas, resting stiffly on revolving metal bases, so giving rise to two cheerful and poetic reinterpretations of the classic armchair.

The *New Antiques* collection (2005) combines vintage and contemporary design in a family of products that have become the manifesto of a distinctive vision of design, focusing on the relations between past and future and seeking to design new classics that will not already be old tomorrow.

The collaboration between Cappellini and Wanders was celebrated in 2011 with an exhibition at the **showroom** in Milan, curated by the Dutch designer. Marking the fifteen years of their partnership and the 1,001 examples of *Knotted Chair* produced, it closed the sales of the first version of this product and led to a second, sure to be followed by many more.

TIMELINE

1946

Enrico Cappellini founds the first Cappellini factory at Carugo.

1977

Giulio Cappellini starts working in the family business, taking it towards more refined projects and materials and building a high-end network of relationships with designers, suppliers and markets.

1980

Cappellini changes its name to Cappellini International Interiors and rapidly becomes a landmark for young designers worldwide. By 1983 it is already exporting 40% of its output.

1986   1987   1988

The contract division is created, but above all the firm presents Shiro Kuramata's *Progetti compiuti* collection, launching the brand on the international scene.

Cappellini becomes a joint stock company comprising the International, Contract and Import divisions. The offering is completed with the "Mondo" brand, which grows out of a collaboration between Giulio Cappellini and Paola Navone.

With the presentation of Jasper Morrison's *Thinking Man's Chair*, Cappellini demonstrates his ability to anticipate trends and fashions.

1989 1994 1996

Beginning of *Progetto Oggetto*, the collection by Jasper Morrison and James Irvine. Cappellini moves into a bigger factory at Arosio to house the growing production needs.

Opens the Magazzini Cappellini space on Via Monte Napoleone in Milan. "Mondo" becomes part of the Cappellini brand.

Achille Castiglioni curates the first retrospective exhibition on Cappellini at the Museum für Angewandte Kunst in Cologne.

1997   2000   2001

The Milan showroom opens in Via Santa Cecilia: a new store called simply "Cappellini," marking an aesthetic and conceptual turning point in the brand's communication.

At the Fuorisalone in Milan, Cappellini exhibits for the first time in the Superstudio factory space.

The first international showroom opens in Paris.

2004   2005   2014

Cappellini joins
the *Poltrona Frau Group*
project.

Cappellini showrooms start
to open around the world:
New York, Los Angeles,
Miami, Manila ...

Cappellini becomes part
of Haworth Group.

AND WHAT'S NEXT?

Design
Heartfelt

Translation
Richard Sadleir

www.electa.it

Distributed in English throughout the World
by Rizzoli international Publications Inc.
300 Park Avenue South
New York, NY 10010, USA

ISO 9001
Mondadori Electa S.p.A. is certified for the Quality
Management System by Bureau Veritas Italia S.p.A.,
in compliance with UNI EN ASO 9001: 2008.

This book respects the environment
The paper used was produced using wood from forests managed
to strict environmental standards; the companies involved
guarantee sustainable production certified environmentally.

This volume was printed at Elcograf S.p.A.,
Via Mondadori 15, Verona
Printed in Italy